DATE			

REVOLUTION

REVOLUTION

THE YEAR I FELL IN LOVE AND WENT TO JOIN THE WAR

DEB OLIN UNFERTH

HENRY HOLT AND COMPANY   NEW YORK

Henry Holt and Company, LLC
Publishers since 1866
175 Fifth Avenue
New York, New York 10010
www.henryholt.com

Henry Holt® and 🏛® are registered trademarks of
Henry Holt and Company, LLC.

The names of some individuals have been changed.

Distributed in Canada by H. B. Fenn and Company Ltd.

Library of Congress Cataloging-in-Publication Data

Unferth, Deb Olin.
    Revolution : the year I fell in love and went to join the war / Deb Olin Unferth.—1st ed.
        p. cm.
    ISBN 978-0-8050-9323-0
    1. Unferth, Deb Olin—Travel—Central America.   2. Central America—Description
and travel.   3. Authors, American—21st century—Biography.   I. Title.
PS3621.N44Z46 2011
813'.6—dc22
[B]   2010023471

First Edition 2011

Designed by Kelly S. Too

Printed in the United States of America
1   3   5   7   9   10   8   6   4   2

For Comrade Robert Unferth

REVOLUTION

PART ONE

THE NEW WORLD

MCDONALD'S

I had food in my heart and mind that morning. My parents had said they'd pick George and me up at the border and take us anywhere we wanted to eat. I wanted to go to McDonald's. My father thought that was funny. Part of his story for a long time was how the first place I wanted to go when I came back from fomenting the Communist revolution was McDonald's. Hey, to me at that moment, McDonald's looked pretty good. We'd seen McDonald's in Mexico, of course, and Honduras and other places, but we hadn't been able to afford it. Now, approaching the border, I was thinking about that lighted menu board. I was thinking about how I already knew what the food I ordered would look like. I knew what the French fries would look like, what the containers would look like, although I'd never been to that particular McDonald's. I knew what I'd get when I got a sundae. That seemed like a neat and attractive trick to me now. There would be toilet paper in the bathrooms. And soap. There were the little songs on TV, the McDonald's songs that people all over the world knew and I had sung when I was a kid, the Big Mac chant, the Hamburglar. George was asleep beside me, had slept through the last seven hours of desert. "George, wake up," I said. "We're going to McDonald's."

POPULAR PRIEST

My boyfriend and I went to join the revolution.

We couldn't find the first revolution.

The second revolution hired us on and then let us go.

We went to the other revolutions in the area—there were several—but every one we came to let us hang around for a few weeks and then made us leave.

We ran out of money and at last we came home.

I was eighteen. That's the whole story.

George and I were walking through a shantytown. Two weeks into Mexico, the beginning of our trip, and we were outside Mexico City. An American priest walked ahead. He was saying hello to people and taking their hands. He was saying good-bye to them and waving. *Que te vaya bien. Adiós. Dios te bendiga.* They chimed back. We walked a long way, following this priest.

It was 1987, and at that time these little liberation theology institutes were set up all over Latin America, "popular churches," they were called, short chapels with small gardens, places for people to get together and help usher in the revolution. The priests were in charge and they could be from anywhere—South America, Spain, the States—but most were from down the street. We liked to drop in when we found these setups. We interviewed whoever happened to be hanging around and we borrowed books from their shelves and got the people to take us out. We liked to get the scoop.

So we'd met this priest at his *instituto* and he'd brought us to the shantytown. He was doing some work, fixing up some floors. He thought we just might like to see.

When you think of a shantytown, you imagine a few square blocks of board and tin, some chickens running through, but it's a whole city, a thousand thin paths, kilometers and kilometers of housewives standing outside askew miniature-sized houses, not a window pane in sight, the air moist and buzzing.

"These people are born and die here," the priest was telling us. "They have no way to get out." He raised his hand to show us where they had to stay.

"Well, at least they've got their little houses," I said. I was impressed with how tidy it all was. "Some have less than that."

The priest looked over at me.

Then he was gone. Just like that. Left George and me standing by a flower of electrical cords coming out of a pole.

We waited a while. Roosters called to each other in the distance. Then we started puzzling around the shacks, trying to find our way back. We were soon lost. We felt stupid and rude walking along, a couple of idiot gringos slapping at the mosquitoes and grinning. We were sad about the priest. Why had he gone away? He'd left us and we deserved it. We'd been bad-mannered. *I'd* been bad-mannered, according to George. George knew better than to say a thing like that. Oh yeah? I said. Then why had the priest left George here with me?

These priests for the liberation. You did not want to mess with them. Latin America was swinging to the left, hoisted on pulleys by these radical priests, and some said the Vatican was to blame. In 1962 the pope had summoned the world's bishops to Rome for the Vatican Two Council, to talk about how to renew the Church, how to be relevant to the laypeople. The story goes that the bishops met each fall for four years. They talked about things like how perhaps they should not say mass in Latin anymore because no one understood it (although the entire conference took place in Latin). Some of the South American bishops and priests thought that one way to renew the Church was to organize the lay into groups, maybe even guerrilla armies, and then rise up and overthrow their governments. Soon a continent of priests was storing weapons and reading Marx in the name of Vatican Two. They turned their churches into revolutionary enclaves and invited students to come live in them like a herd of hippies. Some priests held secret meetings with guerrilla rebels. Some manned radio frequencies that kept tabs on the national guard. And when the skirmishes began, some priests came out shooting. Every day their chapels filled with citizens, and the priests never stopped talking about Vatican Two, the theology of liberation, how the Church was a socialist soldier for the poor, and how grateful they were for this mandate from God. Of course the pope didn't mean to produce an infantry of gun-touting South American priests, and he said so, but it was too late.

Late for the pope, but early for George and me. This priest was the first of his kind, we'd found. We walked, lost, through the shanty-town. Houses tacked up to each other with clothes hangers, a cobweb of roofs held down with tires. Outhouses winged out over the river. Lightless rooms, cardboard town. We began getting upset at seeing how poor the people were, now that we were looking more carefully. Ladies and kids stopped us and pointed in different directions, laughing behind their hands. A few folks followed us. We handed out all of our bills. We didn't see how we would ever find our way back. George was taking us in circles.

Oh, right, he said, *he* was taking us in circles, perfect. We began to panic.

Suddenly the priest was there, stepped out in front of us. Ho ho. He'd stopped in to look at a floor he and some friends had put in. Lost track of us.

What, had we been nervous about getting stuck here? he wondered. About not being able to get out?

"Okay, okay, we get it already," we said, though we did not.

LONG YEAR FOR WAR

We had wanted to go to Cuba, but we didn't know how to get there. George and I had very little money and we weren't resourceful, and it was illegal to go, which was awkward. Besides, there was no action there anymore. Just parades and congratulations and prisoners. Nicaragua had a very good revolution too. They'd won their revolution, for one thing, and they were in the papers all the time, and we could ride the bus there. They also had Russians.

The other revolutions—in El Salvador and Panama, in Guatemala, in Honduras—weren't revolutions proper, more like civil wars, military coups, and armed uprisings. They straggled along with their broken tanks and their camps in the jungle. We believed their revolutions were on the way.

Nineteen eighty-seven was a big year for war in Central America. Still, it took George and me a while to find any. We rode through Mexico on bus rides that lasted eighteen hours, twenty-two hours, twenty-six hours. We passed through Guatemala, where we had to fight our way through the tourists just to see a little scrap of the land. The tourists crowded together like shrubs, trying not to get knocked over. Mostly in Guatemala we were herded by heavily armed soldiers along a well-worn track that took us from pretty spot to pretty spot (look at the Indians! buy their amusing costumes to take home for yourself! ride a wooden boat across a glassy lake!).

People didn't have the details on Guatemala yet. We heard about the killings but we didn't know the extent and the scale. Or maybe we did know and chose not to understand. A couple of years later, when we began to hear so much about the death squads, the scorched earth policy, the tens of thousands of dead, the tens of thousands fleeing the country, I had a sick feeling of knowledge. A massacre, an exodus, going on all around us, had been for years, and still going on after we'd gone, and we saw none of it. We saw a few tattered labor protests, Indians sitting on cardboard in the plaza. Mostly we saw soldiers. Soldiers were in all the shops and banks, on the buses and in the cafés. There were pageants of them on the street. They stopped taxis and leaned in the windows. *"Papeles,"* they said every minute or two. They held machine guns and wore camouflage uniforms, high black boots, helmets, strings of bullets across their chests. On their belts they carried clubs, pistols, Mace, hand grenades.

They were small and young and cute, like toy soldiers. Many only came up to my mouth. They stood and looked at us in moody silence. Poked at the pages of my passport. Sometimes they would pose for a picture.

In those days the Guatemalans still thought they owned Belize or thought they owned it more than they think they own it now, so many of us secretly felt that Belize didn't count. In any case Belize didn't have a revolution. But we went to have a look.

These were the days before the Peace Corps had been let back into the country. The days before Belize had even kicked the Peace Corps out. These were the original Peace Corps days, the days that led to their expulsion from Belize. They were all over the place, the Peace Corps volunteers, drunk in hammocks, lying on the sidewalks. "Hang on, man," they called to us. "Want a smoke?" George and I picked our steps over them on the way to the bus station.

Our main ambition was to help the revolution. George and I wanted jobs, what we called "revolution jobs," but it turned out that few people wanted to hire us and if they did, they almost immediately fired us.

But he and I also conducted interviews. This was his idea, and he was in charge. We started in Mexico and interviewed people clear down to the Panama Canal, dozens of people—politicians, priests, organizers. We brought a bagful of tapes with rock music on them and recorded over the tapes one by one with a hand-held cassette tape recorder. Some people gave us only twenty minutes—the press secretary of Guatemala (with his fake, thin clown smile), the minister of culture of Nicaragua (who wore a beret indoors). The strays—the artist, the small-town priest, the local Native American—would talk for hours if we let them (if George let them). In Nicaragua everyone wanted to be interviewed, top people in the government and church. The taxi drivers wanted to be interviewed. The kids wanted to be interviewed. Their fathers wanted to be interviewed. In Bluefields, Nicaragua, we interviewed the mayor of the city, the leader of the Miskito tribe, the soldiers who had provided military escort to that part of the country. In El Salvador no one wanted to be interviewed. We got only four interviews—one with a painter, a few with some priests—but no one in the government would talk to us or even look at us. We went to the Casa Presidencial in San Salvador every day for weeks and couldn't get near the place. The guards told us that the entire government was on vacation. Every day they told us this. "Still on vacation," they said, spreading their hands. "*¿Lo crees?* Can you believe it?"

"No, I cannot believe that," said George.

I don't know what happened to all those tapes. When we came back to the States, we had them first in plastic bags on the floor by the door of our apartment. Later I recall them sitting in a couple of broken boxes. After that, I'm not sure. Neither of us ever listened to them again, as far as I know.

SEND-OFF

I knew my mother and father were not going to let me join the revolution, so I didn't tell them. I sent them a letter from Mexico. I wrote the letter in Nogales on the American side of the border, then I crossed the border so I could mail it from the Nogales post office on the Mexican side. The letter was short and went something like:

> Dear Mom and Dad,
> I am writing you from Mexico. I'm sorry to tell you in this way, but I've left school and am going to help foment the revolution. I am a Christian now and I have been called by God. Due to the layout of the land, we are taking the bus.

My father still talks about it. "She told us nothing," he says. "We had no idea. I open the mailbox and there's a letter from Mexico saying she's off to foment the revolution."

He's been telling it the same way all these years. He used to shout it, "My own daughter told me nothing!" and point at me— there she is, the traitor, the nutcase, the smartass.

Later he said it sadly, shaking his head: "I had no idea."

Even later he said it with pride. His loony girl, a bit like him. Do you know he once owned a Communist bookstore?

Now he tells it like an old joke. "So one day I open the mail-box..."

Before we left, George brought the stuff we would need up out of his parents' basement—backpacks, insect repellent, flashlights, soap, some philosophical books about the Bible. I threw my other belongings away and I did it happily because at the revolution I would need only what I could carry. We put our money together (we each had a thousand dollars). We got shots and a bottle of malaria pills.

George told his mother our plan. We sat at her kitchen table while he explained. She listened and then took out some pot holders for us to take along and bookmarks with pictures of God on them. She had the face of captive royalty, the voice of something gentle in a cage. She told me to memorize the Bible bit by bit and then to write it down at the revolution and send it to her in the mail. We left the pot holders behind, but she also gave us a very large, very heavy canister of vitamin powder that we never used but carried for months and months over borders, on boats, through storms.

George's father was there too that day but he didn't speak. I never saw him speak, in fact, and it seemed to me that no one had. The man sat looking angry, alone on the sofa in the living room. He rose only to come through the kitchen on his way to the door.

The year George and I went was nearly the end of the revolution, but the way it looked to us, we were arriving at the very beginning. A new world order. Everybody in the world was talking about the revolution, how it was coming over the ocean, it was floating up through Texas. It would spread over America. People were writing their ideas in the papers. But two years later the

Berlin Wall came down and soon after that the Sandinistas were gone, the Cold War was over, and the guerrillas in El Salvador handed in their arms, put down their names on a peace accord. By the time we arrived, the Communist decay had set in, but we didn't know. There were a lot of people like us on the scene.

PART TWO

CIVIL WAR

BODIES

George and I were on a bus headed into El Salvador, a secret bus in the middle of the night. Soft bundles of people sat on each seat, but the space was so voiceless and dim, you'd think we were all gone and the bus rode emptily along. And yet the bus was heavy, pulling itself up hills around bends. You could feel the brakes holding back the weight as we coasted down. I was angry with George. "This is not going to work," I told him. Dark windows, the weird sound of cicadas. An occasional wet branch hit the glass. George said nothing.

The bus shuddered through a downshift and rolled to a stop. We'd run only a few kilometers over the border so far. The people in the seats around us began murmuring and shifting at the windows because out on the road we could see men with machine guns filed out in front of the bus and walking along the sides.

It was too bad that we wanted to take the bus to El Salvador. We weren't allowed on the roads. No one was. No foreigners were even allowed in the country at that time, unofficially—save a few special exceptions, and there certainly wasn't anything special about George and me, but we'd managed to get in. We'd lined up a job, although that hadn't gotten us in. Then we'd been persistent. Long after the other gringos had given up, had gone staggering off to Honduras (visit the islands! see the *ruinas*, cheap!), we were still there at the consulate, every day, with our passports, but that hadn't done it either. Finally we figured out a trick they were playing on us involving the papers we needed to get into the country. And even then we hadn't gotten normal visas. El Salvador wasn't giving out plain come-as-you-are visas—what do you think this is, a party? We had overland visas with a three-day window for entrance, which meant you had to come through the land, not drop in from the sky or swim the sea, and you had three days to make it. But either by coincidence (unlikely) or in yet another round of diversions, they'd given us the visas on the very day the rebels of El Salvador—the FMLN, the leftist guerrillas of the mountains—had announced on the radio that their plan was to halt any vehicle they found on the road and blow it up. This was called a "paro," a "stop," because things that move stop moving in the face of threatened destruction. Buses, cars, trucks, everyone stopped and stayed home, the roads were tenantless as housetops. We'd gone anyway. (Not my idea.)

The FMLN, the Farabundo Martí National Liberation Front. Named for Farabundo Martí, that Marxist, radical, peasant leader of the thirties, whose greatest achievement was the botched revolt of 1932—half aborted at the last moment, half carried out in confusion, entirely crushed by the National Guard and resulting in thirty thousand deaths. He rose again in the form of these rebels who took his name, a clear vote for human striving over (or in the absence of?) strength, proof of the poetic (quixotic?) mind of the Salvadoran campesino.

George had a plan as to what we would say if the FMLN stopped the bus. I spoke better Spanish. I'd spent time in Mexico as a child. I would do the talking. The theory was that the guerrillas would shoot Americans or take them hostage. I was supposed to explain to the guerrillas that George and I were on their side and that we'd been trying to find them. That we had meant to put ourselves in their way. We wanted to interview them with our tape recorder and take their pictures. We wanted to join them. But I didn't want to do the talking. I'd mess it up and get us killed and then get blamed for it.

"This is never going to work," I said.

The men on the ground strayed around the sides, stringing the bus, moving like night creatures. We couldn't see their garb, only their figures and the silhouette of their weapons pointed up. Then the front door sighed open and the people around us quieted. The men got on. At last we could see: they had on military uniforms. It was not the FMLN. It was the *other* teenagers with enormous machine guns, the ones who happened *not* to be assigned to attack civilians today, the militia, checking *papeles*, searching bags, asking questions. We all got off the bus.

We found machine guns disturbing in El Salvador, more so than in Guatemala, where we heard only twigs of rumors of killings. But in El Salvador people were always talking about bodies—the bodies found nearby, the lists passing around of the bodies by name, the lists hidden in a film canister and run over the mountains to Honduras, the lists read aloud in the U.S. Congress, and the counts made, the separate counts for the same set of bodies: the militia's count, the embassy's count, the FMLN's, the villagers', the counts reported in the papers—"two found with hands removed," "ninety-six found beneath a church." The counts made no sense, they were off by a hundred, two hundred. They always had to be redone, but already the bodies were gone, no one knew where. The number of bodies was tracked like the stock market.

Is the number of bodies growing or shrinking? Over the last year, has it declined by half or risen a third? The count was affected by invisible forces. A flock of birds rising and falling. The number was out of control, a wind coming up in the night, the way those bodies appeared on the streets or in the fields—not that we saw the bodies themselves, we only heard about them, the numbers of them, attached to phrases like "totally false," "a fabrication of subversives," "a massacre."

We were standing alongside the bus. It was maybe the tenth or eleventh time we'd had to get off the bus and now it was nearly dawn. Every half hour, all night, the bus had stopped and we'd had to get off, over and over. I was saying to George that I'd *told* him this wasn't going to work. Then the soldiers said, "You two stay here," and they waved everyone else back on the bus. There were about six or seven soldiers. They took all of our things out of our bags and lined them up on the ground. They took away our map. "Forbidden." They gestured with their machine guns for us to pick up our belongings and explain what each item was. They asked questions with their machine guns. "You," they said, pointing at me with a machine gun. "What are you doing in El Salvador?"

"*Turismo*," I said. (I'd been told that if a soldier points a gun at you, you should always say "*turismo*.")

It was still dark, but you could feel the light on its way. "What's in this bottle?" they said. "What is this book? What does it say? Read it. Read it aloud. Translate." They were passing around our passports. They spilled the plastic bag of cassette tapes on the ground. "What's this?" They took one of the cassette tapes and put it into our cassette player. We didn't know for a moment if they had picked one with music or interviews on it, and George looked very grave. They turned on the cassette player. They had picked one with music on it.

"Sing," they said. "Sing along."

We sang. It was a song about a transvestite who loves another transvestite, or maybe only one of them is a transvestite. George and I sang about how girls can be boys and boys can be girls and how mixed up that is. A sad song with deep tones. Behind us the sun was coming up.

"Translate," the soldiers said with their machine guns. "What does it say?"

"Love song," George told them, and they did something that looked like a laugh.

TYPICAL MAN

I met George when I was seventeen and a freshman in college at a large state school in a large state, the entire student body united behind rituals involving their sports activities. I was new to that part of the country, had grown up in Chicago, but George had been raised nearby. He'd grown up in the western middle of America, in the kind of neighborhood where most people don't have passports and no one speaks any language other than the one they'd been raised to suspect was God's favorite. George had played tag among these people, had attended their schools, dated their daughters, and so by all counts he should have been like them, but he wasn't, or he didn't seem so to me.

I became his girlfriend at a protest. I'd heard the chanters and the bullhorn from my window, and I'd come out of the dorm and over the grass to watch. I'd never seen a protest up close before. It was one of those anti-CIA protests of the Cold War eighties, back when the CIA still made it serious business to come to campus once a year to interview possible recruits, and the hippies left over from the sixties showed up to exercise their right to object.

I remember seeing George that day. I'd met him once before. He was a friend of a friend from the dorm, and we'd talked one night at a concert. Now he was sifting through the protesters toward me, the hippies swaying. They looked drab and disarranged beside their cop counterparts in fine suits and unhappy helmets, standing in a line. Against this blur, George was young and shining. He shifted through the assortment of people, sliding around them. He came over to the tree I stood under, leaves falling all around. He had blue-green eyes and the sort of blond hair that blonds call not blond. He held up his fist to me like a microphone and asked me what I wanted to say.

George had an odd system of rules. He didn't believe in paying bills. Phone bills, library fines, gas bills. It was a principle for him: never pay bills. Corporations were evil, rich, foolish to trust him. Around that time credit card companies first began handing out cards to students. He thought this was funny. He called it free money. He signed up for several credit cards, spent up to the limit, and threw the bills away. At first I didn't know how this was going to work out for him, but it wasn't as bad as you'd think. Bills piled up and floated away, and more appeared to replace them. Yet he never refused someone money if asked, even if he himself really needed it (which was always), so he was usually broke. It was what made me fall in love with him: his disregard for rules other than his own. He simply didn't care about money, possessions, sleep, food. I found this daring and visionary. I wanted to be like that too.

He had a coterie of friends since childhood who were protective, fearful for him. "Oh, give it here," they'd say, dropping a twenty on the counter, "I'll pay for his." Never resentful, they acted as if George had done them some quiet deed long ago and now they were in his debt, or—on his more annoying days—as if he were the kid brother whose father on his deathbed had charged

them with his care. Maybe to them he seemed hopeless or muddled. You could not have a regular conversation with the guy. He
had no reaction to chitchat about sports, school, snow. He never
swore, never took drugs. At a party he was the one in the corner
bending the lamp into strange shapes. He wasn't outgoing and he
wasn't a leader. He was a prankster, but all his pranks were private jokes. I was the only one who laughed. To me, George was
spectacular, misunderstood, brilliant. He was a senior and he
studied continuously, four hours a night, and he never missed a
class. At a school like ours, this was deranged. He went in for
physics, philosophy, and math. Amid the psych majors, the com-
munications minors, boys sunk in bean bags watching ball, no
one understood what he was talking about. He was just smarter
than everyone else.

"Genius," was how I put it then. "He's a *genius.*" I felt that I'd
come from a long line of genius men. The women in my family
fell in love with geniuses, was how I understood it.

"I believe he might be the real thing," I told my friends from
home on the phone. "A true *genius.*"

He and I both had checked jackets for some reason. The jackets
more or less matched, and we rarely took them off. We walked
around campus, jabbering to each other in those jackets. Whatever few scraps of friends I'd begun to make in the dorms I
immediately forgot. Until I met George I'd found my new college
life that had been set up for me boring, excruciatingly so, and the
people who were supposed to be my new college friends by far the
most boring element in it: smiley, well-built women—skiers, run-
ners, blondes. They were eager to describe their organizational
achievements—their schedules, their sports activities, their boy-
friends, their matching heart mugs and flower shower buckets. So
if I wasn't with George, I wasn't with anyone. He and I would

meet up at four o'clock each day and, before our long nights of homework, go scrounging for food. I had a meal ticket, but I didn't want to be away from him for the time it took to eat.

At first we slept in the physics building, a tower that rose high over the campus. He held a key to the top floor. A lounge of couches stood under a line of tall windows. He was living there, had given up his room in an apartment—or he was about to, I don't recall the exact timing. I only recall his inconvenient, complex housing plan, which involved him moving his belongings every few days. But he was putting one over on the school, he told me. They'd left themselves open. He could have it all for free. Late at night we walked through the physics tower, perfecting the housing plan, how he'd eat, the rooftop barbeques.

For a while it was just he and I kidding around, laughing at our own jokes, but soon it became a powerful passion. It was us against them, and "they" were anybody, everybody—whoever they were, they were out there, and we were against them, jokingly.

He had a huge number of brothers, most of whom lived on the nearby flatland of flags and rectangles of lawn. He brought me to meet them one by one. The oldest of them had been a hippie and the rest thought that was cool. They were sorry they had missed out. They still listened to the music and wore the floppy hats and talked about how the oldest had had all the luck. The first few brothers were religious and smart about it, studying philosophy and theology. George was the last of this group. The very final brother, the youngest, the "baby," hated all the other brothers. He wanted to be a cop and put the other brothers in jail.

The two oldest brothers knew how to fix cars, how to read a mountain map, and they taught the other brothers their skills.

They wore beards and gave advice. They played father to the younger brothers among them. The father himself didn't behave like a father. I don't know why. It was a deep wound in the family, the father. He never spoke and he wore a sarcastic expression on his face, a combination of irritation and mock surprise. The brothers and the mother conferred in low tones about how he might react to things they wanted to do. When he was in the house, everyone felt his presence, although he was never in the same room.

I have photos of George and me hitchhiking through New Mexico over Christmas, the two of us standing on the road. I have photos of the people who picked us up. There's the prison guard, the truck driver, the lady with the dog. There's the town Truth or Consequences, where we couldn't find a ride. We look ludicrously happy, thin and young and grinning. I'm carrying a camera that looks like a gun.

By spring we stopped going to the physics tower. He moved into my room in the dorm, brought his books and a duffel of clothes. We got in big trouble for that. The resident assistants called us into the office. The dorm administrators called us into another office. They said I was on dorm warning. They said we were both kicked out. George said not to worry. He said we would live on the quad in a tent (students were doing that—as a show of solidarity with South Africa). He said not to worry, we would get blankets and camp out in the fields (Fidel Castro, Central Park, 1960, until Malcolm X came and carried him to Harlem). It was a problem, a big problem, and just when I was beginning to wonder (and maybe worry) how this was all going to play out (blankets in the fields? now how would that work?), suddenly it wasn't a problem anymore because George said we would drop out of school and join the revolution.

I said okay.

George had been to Mexico and Guatemala—just once, the year before he and I met. At school he'd met a Guatemalan student whom I never knew and who had talked George into coming with him home. I believe he needed an extra driver. As far as I could gather, George had spent the entire three weeks drunk. I am amazed that he had been such a typical gringo on that trip, drunk, waving his pesos at a bartender. But I suppose if you put anyone in a certain context, they could look typical, even if they aren't. Maybe he's sitting somewhere looking typical right now. Maybe for years now he's been looking that way, and no one around him knows who he really is.

Once, in our first months together, George and I somehow came up with a car and we drove to the border of Utah. At the border sign we pulled over and pushed the car across with our hands so we could say, "Whew, we pushed the car to Utah last night."

I don't know, maybe that's a typical thing to do. Maybe that's the point: he was just a typical guy in a typical place, and he made choices, and each choice changed him, and each change began to close off other possibilities, seal shut other rooms, exclude other people he might become, one by one, until he could no longer be anything but what he was.

I'm not sure what it was about that first trip to Guatemala that made him want to go back, but he did. That man, that typical drunk gringo in Guatemala, had emerged from the bar, sobering in the light, brushing off his shirt, waving away his comrades, and had taken a new walk—not the one he took with me, that was just more of the same, minus the drinking—but the one after ours, a walk he would never return from, not really, not because he didn't want to and not because he wasn't allowed to, but because he couldn't. A typical man is capable of that.

SPANISH

It turns out that no one in my family is a genius, male or female. I understood that later, another broken myth tossed in an old box with Santa. But all of us are fairly smart, can do our times tables, can follow installation instructions, and most of us can speak Spanish. Unlike George, I'd spent a good deal of time in Mexico growing up, starting from the age of four. My grandparents had a house in Mexico, and my first words in Spanish were *"Leche chocolate, por favor"* and *"¿Dónde están los gatitos?"* so obviously I knew what was important.

Houses in Mexico were cheap at that time and my grandfather bought one for my grandmother. Each fall he packed her off to Mexico, and she drove from Chicago to Cuernavaca and then waited for the rest of us to show up on airplanes when we could get away. This was before the Free Trade Agreement, and Grandmother told me solemn stories about how the officials would stop her car and take away her place mats. Other people came to the house too, Mexicans and Americans. Grandfather invited them, or someone did. We all hung around the garden and swam in the pool. I have photos from that time of the men and women lying around on towels in the grass. It was the seventies and they looked pretty groovy in their haircuts and clothes. I don't know who those people were. I used to say they were artists. I used to tell people that painters and writers would come stay with us in Mexico, but I don't think that's right. I think they were business associates of my grandfather. They liked to play board games with me and do thousand-piece puzzles, or at least they pretended to. They left behind books that I read and didn't understand. *Call It Sleep. Fear of Flying. Lolita.*

Behind my grandparents' house there were no other houses yet. I walked through the fields back there with the woman who did the laundry. Across the street from us lived an old blind man alone in a large house. My father would send my brother and me over to visit him. My father felt nervous and sad if we didn't go every few days. I believe this was because my father is afraid of death. To get us to visit, my father told us the old man would give us cookies and ice cream. That was a lie. The man never gave us cookies or ice cream and I think my father understood that.

The old man talked about the War for hours. My brother and I were trapped. All I could do was dream of getting away. I never understood whose side he was on. He had one picture of himself with Goebbels, one of himself with Himmler, and one with Churchill. He talked about Nazi Germany for hours and hours. He spoke six languages, but with us he mostly spoke English and Spanish. The old man was blind, but he knew where the pictures were on his walls and would bring us over to them and make us stand there. He could also play the ukulele. He was the most boring man I've ever known. My brother thought he was fascinating. We visited him all the time until one year we came back and he was dead.

JOB

George and I arrived at the orphanage just in time for the all-night prayer vigil, which was our luck.

"All-night prayer vigil, what is that?" I said. We'd made it to El Salvador, had gotten off the paro bus and arrived at the orphanage only a few minutes before. I was tired and dead ready to eat. We stood in the entry in our backpacks.

"A vigil. You know, prayer?" said Hermana Mana.

A detachment of orphans raveled themselves around my legs. "What for?"

"*Por la guerra.* For the war. Have you heard we have a war going on in El Salvador?"

I looked at George. He was bent over, studying a regiment of orphans who had settled at his feet. Frankly I didn't think that praying all night was going to help, not to mention how smart is it to keep eight-year-olds up past ten? Stay up all night? What a horrendous idea. God had ears to hear just as well in the morning.

Hermana Mana folded her arms. "Or do you not believe in the power of prayer?" She was not a nun. We were just supposed to call her Hermana Mana.

George was walking as if in galoshes, a band of orphans wrapped on. "Okay, okay," he said. "Let's all pray for the war."

Our first revolution job was in El Salvador, where there was a civil war, not a revolution. (I was only half clear on the difference: it appeared that it was just an insurrection or at most a civil war until it was won, at which point it became a revolution.) During the civil war in El Salvador villages were being taken apart—bombed or scorched—and the villagers were being rounded up and killed by military forces because it was assumed that the villagers wanted to rise up against the military and overthrow the government. But sometimes a mother and a father would be killed and a child would be left over, hidden, who would come out later and walk to another village, maybe with a little brother or a sister or a friend by the hand. So an orphanage had been set up just outside the war zone. The kids rode on local buses from the orphanage over the hills each day to a village school and then they rode back, and everybody agreed not to bomb or shoot them, even though these kids were nascent insurgents, sympathizers by birth, so some said, and in fact the military did bomb them, just the once—killed the kitchen, before we arrived—after all, the place was filled with a bunch of budding FMLN guerrilla fighters, so what did they expect?

The problem is then the war moved over a little, so the orphanage was right in the middle of it and then the paro began, so the buses stopped running and the kids couldn't go to school or leave the premises at all.

This is about the time George signed us up for the job.

"Who keeps kids up all night?" I whispered to George while we put down our stuff, the orphans waiting behind us. "An all-night vigil. Is this insane?"

"Could you just go along with it?" he whispered back. He turned and smiled at the group.

We all crowded into a classroom-like room, rectangles covering the ceiling and floor. We took seats on the linoleum. George sat on the other side of the room with a stack of orphans in his lap, and a couple of the littler ones crawled into my lap too. We lit candles and sang songs to God. "Please take care of everybody, God," we prayed. "You are so wonderful, God." Outside the shooting started up. That surprised me. I hadn't realized how close we were to the fighting. It sounded like the shots were right outside. Explosions shook the floor and the children began crying. Suddenly I could see the sense in an all-night vigil. These were children whose villages had been burned to the ground, their parents pulled away, shot or tortured, while they hid in a bush and watched. I had no idea what I was supposed to do. I was terrified. This is what George had brought me here for? The first night of my civil war job I vomited four times.

PROJECTS

That week at the orphanage, George instituted early morning exercise, mandatory for all the boys. They loved it. He held sports games after lunch, games that involved throwing balls and catching them. The girls could join in too. Everyone wanted to throw the ball to George and wanted George to throw it back to them. He came up with a system for the boys to bring water from the river that made this chore somehow fun, or so it seemed from the laughter I could hear on the path.

I came up with projects too. I had the idea of planting a garden. I had done something like this in the second grade—not outside, but in little cups at our desks, some indestructible vine. There was plenty of dirt and grass around. "Go ahead," said Hermana Mana. She didn't point out that these kids had come from agrarian villages and were not going to be impressed by a few plants the way kids from the city were (i.e., me). A man came in a car once a week to bring supplies. He agreed to let me ride with him to town so I could buy seeds. I came back happy with my industriousness. I found a place for a garden and was crouching on the ground, ready to direct the orphans. A few stood around me and looked on. George strolled over. "What are you planting?"

I held up the packages.

"They didn't have any vegetable seeds?" He took the packages and read them slowly, one by one. "You think they have a shortage of flowers?"

I put down my little spade.

"No, no," he said, handing back the packages. "By all means. Bring on the flowers. I'll sit right here and watch."

I decided to try to teach the girls how to read. Now, these orphans went to school every day except during a paro, I knew that, and so I should have known that those of reading age knew how to read. I had an idea of orphanages in my mind and of what one does at them and that idea included giving classes in how to read. The children were too polite to tell me that they knew how to read, so they sat there pretending not to.

I was an astonishment of a teacher. They were all reading within days. In fact they could read better than I could. I'd had a few classes of Spanish but I hadn't paid much attention (my brother and I held that Spanish class was not cool). Mostly I'd learned Spanish by speaking. The orphans had to keep correcting me. We'd recite the alphabet together and each time we all faltered on the fourth letter because in Spanish the alphabet goes, A, B, C, CH, D. . . . I knew CH counted as a letter, but I kept forgetting. We'd start out together: A, B, C, but on the fourth letter, the orphans would say CH and I would say D and then they would say D and I would say E and we would all be confused for a moment before falling silent. Don't ask me why this happened more than once.

I decided to teach them English. This went extraordinarily badly. They couldn't learn a word of English. I must have been a truly terrible teacher because for several days in a row I grilled them over and over on the simplest things. Hello. How are you. I am seven years old. And they couldn't understand at all. They couldn't pronounce the words. They couldn't remember the phrases. They didn't understand the English-learning games I'd come up with. It was an embarrassment for us all.

THE EVANGELICALS

They were religious at the orphanage.

I'd been an atheist Jew when I met George—have I mentioned that? But all he had to do was say he was a Christian for a while and soon I was saying I was a Christian too. I don't know how to explain that. I suppose it's a good thing George came along and not someone worse because it's possible that I was ready to take on any irregular person or object headed my way.

I liked being a Christian, seeing the beautiful in the ugly and attributing it to a Thing higher than myself. I was no longer looking at the world alone. I could turn my head and wink at Someone, the One who put it there, like a couple so long together that they each know what the other is thinking. I liked how confusing Christianity was, how it required so much explaining: why we'd sip blood, why we'd pretend to sip blood, why God would punish us, why He'd punish someone else and pretend it was us, and so on. The enormous mystery of God was much more congruous with my disorienting experience of the world than the arrogant certainty of atheism.

George and I were not the kind of Christians you see asking for money on TV, the ones handing out pamphlets at airports, not the born-again, sky-bound kind. We were Calvinist-Marxist-Kierkegaardian Christians. To explain this in a way that reflects how I understood it: Calvinists are predeterminists. They hold that God has already decided our fate. You can pray or strive or whatever you like, but in the end there isn't much you can do about a thing. The Marxist liberation theologians, on the other hand, believe that humans determine their own fate. We must take (armed) action on Earth, seize the promised land, crush heaven onto the planet. I found these two combined incoherent, but luckily they were balanced by a dose of Kierkegaard: Yes, you're right, the thing is absurd. Who could believe such nonsense. But if it made sense, what would be so special about faith?

At the orphanage they weren't any of those. They were evangelicals: Let's just sit down and pray, by God. Maybe we'll get what we want by pleading and flattery.

The evangelical takeover was just beginning in Central America. You'd run into them in groups—evangelicals huddled under a bridge, evangelicals singing through a rainstorm. You'd hear them in the night far off, their tambourines ringing from their church-shacks.

George's mother's church, back in the U.S. West, was evangelical, and that church sponsored our orphanage. One of her pastors had lined up our job for us. In the States, the mid-eighties were the sunny celebrity days of the megachurches: Jim Bakker and his Christian amusement park, Tammy Faye and her eye makeup, the sour Falwell, the limousines they all rode around in, the public scandals in the papers. George's mother's church was an offshoot of those. Her church was a monstrosity, so ugly you couldn't help but wonder how this had happened, whether the architect had dismantled a shopping mall and reassembled it as a giant bin for storing humans for suspicious purposes. The lobby was building-sized. The parking lot was town-sized. The gift shop was a warehouse of crap. Inside the church thousands of cheap plush seats multiplied up into the balconies. The pastors were rich. They wore rich people's clothes and rich people's watches, and you could see them on movie screens overhead, telling about sin and repentance, hours of how to love your neighbor, the intricate details of passing the collection plate, of songs. Once George and I arrived at the orphanage, he couldn't stop talking about it: What were they messing around with all that junk for when here in El Salvador these children barely ate? The orphans ate tortillas and beans for every meal. They grew their own corn. He couldn't get over it. The wastefulness of the church, the very paint they used, twenty dollars a can to put down white lines on a lot to show the idiot Americans how to arrange their cars, twenty dollars that could do so much here.

George and I didn't like the North American evangelicals. Each time we saw them, we made sly jokes and slow getaways. (I singled George's mother out as the sole acceptable American evangelical, but George seemed unsettled on the subject. Around her he displayed a face of determined patience.)

One time, in Guatemala, George and I ran into some of these fellows on the plaza. They're nothing like us, we told each other, because, look, they're all wearing the same outfit—white shirts and white pants. They looked more like each other than like us. And also not like us because they were from Alabama and spoke Spanish with a Southern accent. But we kept a straight face. And there were more of them than us, an entire bus full. They had ridden to Guatemala from Alabama, or maybe they flew and got the bus when they arrived. And they weren't like us because (surprise!) they were actors and dancers. They cleared a little space on the street. They asked the Guatemalan people there if they wouldn't mind moving over just a little. Then they put on a play about Jesus. You weren't supposed to know it was Jesus at first. It was about a king who wore a crown (Styrofoam) and a cape (kings wear capes), and a servant with bare feet who stole or wanted to steal (this part was a little muddy). The punishment for stealing was death (now we figured out where this was going) and the king said he'd rather not have even the poorest of his servants die and that he would take the servant's place (inconvenient domestic policy).

After the play we stood on the street and talked to these evangelicals about God and Guatemala. "We're just bringing the Good News here," they said (because the Guatemalans hadn't heard it).

"Will you come with us?" the evangelicals had asked us. They gestured toward the bus. "Come, come."

In El Salvador it occurred to me that in fact we must have all looked alike to the Guatemalan people watching us. You have to look at a thing carefully to be able to tell it from the others, and you have to know what to look for. Most things are indistinguishable.

A year and a half later, in the final cough of George and me, I had forgotten all about the orphanage, but George was still betrayed by his mother's church. He had the idea that we put a certain bowl by the door of our apartment, a bowl we'd procured from some dying native tribe and carried back over the land to the States somehow without crushing it. The idea was that when a moment arrived that we wanted to go out and spend idle money—a new sweater, dinner out, a show—we would forgo the adventure and instead put the money in the bowl to mail at the end of the month to the orphanage.

I don't know if we ever sent any money. George was in charge of the affair.

HERMANA MANA

She had no patience for me. I was just a bad teenager hanging around the orphanage being bad. "*¿Qué haces?*" she said. She had Salvadoran stubborn eyes and the wind blew her dark curls. When she lifted her arms, the space filled in with children. She disliked me and I was terrified.

"Have you never washed a dish in your life?" she said.

I froze, sponge in hand. (I hadn't or hadn't much. I could put dishes in the dishwasher with the best of them.)

"The girls are going to fetch water. I suppose you've never done that either," she said, as if no one in the United States had to fetch water from the river. (Of course no one did.)

She knew English and spoke it well, but to us she spoke Spanish. If she switched to English with me it meant she really meant business. It meant she was furious.

She loved George. "At last a man has come," she said. She lilted a little in Spanish. "We've been here alone so long and now God has sent us a man." She wore girlish dresses, bare hair knocking around her shoulders. She could pull out a shy grin.

"*Para servirle*, at your service," George said, straightening his shoulders, ready to give a more dramatic demonstration of his worth beyond mere child care.

Yeah, George. That guy clicked into place like a battery. He

was out in the courtyard, tossing a ball around, playing basket-
ball and winning. The orphans wanted him to win, they let him
win. You should have seen him, running around in circles with
the boys. Making them do push-ups. They loved him. It was awful.
The youngest were scared of me. A girl who couldn't pat a tortilla.
Who could barely lift a pail of water. Who couldn't sew. I was a
disaster. I was scared of them too. The oldest were a year younger
than me and ignored me. I was even more afraid of them. I tried
to reach them in our own language—teenage talk—but that too
was a bad setback. My ideas about Christianity were more liberal
than Mana's—I mean, they weren't allowed to dance or wear
makeup, for Christ's sake—and I knew a few things that teenage
girls like to do for fun.

It wasn't going to work out, okay?

It was the bra that brought it to an end. We'd been there only a
couple of weeks. Mana said I had to wear a bra. I said I was flat-
chested and saw no point to it and anyway I didn't even own one.
She said the man with the car would make a special trip to bring
me to a store where I could buy one. I said that was a fine way to
spend money. I said that was a fine way to waste everyone's afternoon. "And you know what?" I said to George. "Who cares. It's
a bra."

"Just borrow a bra from Mana," George said.

(He'd noticed Mana's bra.)

We were in the hallway talking furtively because we were supposed to be demonstrating proper male-around-female behavior,
which was no behavior, which was male-stay-away-from-female
behavior because we'd been foolish enough to admit we weren't
married so we had to stay in separate girls' and boys' houses and
call each other "hermano" and "hermana." Everybody was an
hermano or hermana around there. You didn't have to be a nun.

They all marched around in lines like a movie musical. I couldn't stand to be away from George. That would change later, but at that point to be kept apart was the height of outrage. I walked from room to room, despairing and fuming.

"I don't want to wear a stupid bra," I said.

"Would it really kill you?" said George. "Would you drop dead?"

"Since when are you so interested in bras? Since when do you just follow whatever rule there happens to be? I don't see you wearing a bra."

"She has a lot more to think about than you and your bras."

"Apparently she doesn't," I said.

Mana was alone out there, apart from the local woman who cleaned. She was guardian of some sixty children, shooting going on outside the wall. She didn't even have a car on the premises, let alone a couple of buses in case they had to evacuate. And things were bad. The soldiers were suspicious. They had an eye out for rebel activity, they had their orders. The orphanage was strictly *evangélico* and therefore unpolitical. But every day or two a soldier came to the gate and talked to Mana. She didn't let the soldiers in and they didn't make her, but they were coming around. Maybe they thought she had a few guerrilla fighters hiding in there, but I went all over that orphanage and I never saw any guerrillas. And the kids were wrecks. They screamed in their sleep. Several of them, every night, started screaming when they fell asleep. Some screamed most of the night. You could wake them and hug them and be nice to them and tell them stories or sing a song, but when they went back to sleep, they would start screaming again. You had to just let them scream, otherwise they wouldn't get any sleep and would be tired and cranky the next day. You slept with shooting going on outside and a child next to you screaming.

Mana was young. She must have been under thirty. She had an

education. She could have gone to the States, left that war country. What was she doing there? Was it courage? Loyalty? Hope? It's possible that I've never known any of those, but you'd think I'd at least recognize them.

We had the argument about the bra, and that night I walked into one of the bedrooms and demanded of the girls, "Where in the Bible does it say you have to wear a bra?"

They looked up, wordless, their faces like searchlights.

"Who says God says you have to wear a bra?" I said.

They said nothing. They looked afraid.

That was it. Mana kicked me out. The paro was over by this time. In fact it had been over and started and over by this time. The weekly man came and drove George and me away from the orphanage. He dropped us off on an empty road and left.

OH BROTHER

This might be the place to note that there are fifty-three mountains over fourteen thousand feet in Colorado. I don't know why fourteen thousand feet in particular is an interesting number, but George and his brothers wanted to climb to the top of them all. The brothers had a rather unoriginal nickname for the mountains. They called them "fourteeners." Some of the "fourteeners" had never been climbed before or some such—but that can't be right. How could they know how high a mountain was unless someone had been to the top? But I figured that had to be the case because why else would they want to climb it?

George had taken me up a few fourteeners. The climb took all day, sometimes two days, and there were blizzards, and we'd run out of water, and we'd pass the tree line and not be able to breathe, and still we'd have hours and hours to go. When we reached the top, we'd leap around the boulders up there until we found a metal tube with a pen and a list of names inside. Gasping and freezing, we added our names and then we hurried back down. So that was why people climbed up these things, to write their names down on the list.

Later, when someone would ask what kind of a dumb idea that was, going to El Salvador during the civil war—*their* civil war—I'd think of that.

ON THE ROAD

"Well," I said. "We better figure out how to get out of here."

George and I had on our backpacks. The orphanage driver had driven away.

"How can you be fired from a job that doesn't pay?" George was marveling at this.

A rack of low hills. Prairie pulled out of a sack.

"Which way do you think we should go?" I squinted down the road.

"Didn't you do any babysitting in high school?"

"It wasn't my fault."

"Okay. Whose fault was it then?"

"I never said I wanted to come here."

"Oh, I see." He was really working himself up. He was throwing his arms out and shouting. "I see. It's my fault."

"That's it," I said. "I'm leaving."

"Well, we can't stay here, now can we." He gestured to here: a bowl of blue, a spill of meadow, a road running over a summit. Nothing. Not a pig scratching around. Not an empty soda sideways in the dust.

I turned and started walking.

"Where are you going?" he said.

"Hey," he called. "Where do you think you're going?"

I yelled across the flat of field. "Away from YOU!"

"Fine!"

"I hate you!" I screamed.

"I hate you too!" he screamed back. He walked off in the other direction.

I kept walking. I was so upset I could barely see. I hadn't wanted to go to that stupid orphanage in the first place. It was his idea, always his ideas. I walked on, crying and hiccupping, down one hill and up another. Not even a telephone pole on the horizon. I was angry and ashamed and I hated him with the freshness of wet cement, a new imprint, a hand coming down on my mind and marking it. I shifted my stupid backpack and walked on. Who did he think he was, bringing me to a place like this, the bully? Oh, I'd show him. I imagined myself telling the story to a blurry assemblage of strangers. Defending myself, explaining. "Yes, he just left me there," I was saying to the strangers. "And that's when I went off and joined the revolution for real . . ."

I turned to send up another shout but I was at the saucepan bottom of a hill. My view was blocked, I couldn't see him. Tears began tweezing out again. How was I even supposed to get home?

I kept walking. I came to the top of a hill and looked back. A mat of land. Out along the edge of the sky, a gathering of mountains. Not a town, not a tree in sight. There he was, not moving, a lone coat rack on a hill, the one vertical object. Hot valley air, a windshield's worth of mosquitoes. He was looking toward me. I kept going, but more slowly now. I increased the distance between us by smaller increments. I looked back again. He was walking in my direction. I slowed more. I strolled past thin white birds standing in the fields. He followed, and in this way we went over the hills. Finally I brushed the dust from my dress and turned to face him. Narrow birds took slim steps along the sidelines. He came closer and closer. He stopped.

LOVE

We didn't use the word "love" with each other. We prided ourselves on it. Not for the usual fairy-tale Communist reasons (love is a capitalist prison) (Communists are always so drearily romantic) but for our own fairy-tale reason: we wouldn't say it unless we knew our love would last forever (this was my thinking, of course, true love is eternal, and so on), and though we secretly believed that our love *would* last forever, we were too romantic to say it.

But after the paro, then the orphanage, then my walking away, and then his not abandoning me in the hills, and now the bus that we waited for to carry us away to the capital and the road that we sat on full of bugs, I had my head on my arms. What a selfish, inadequate revolutionary I was. My first civil war job and I'd screwed it up. I felt discardable, disposable. In fact I'd always felt that way, and now that I'd failed so miserably at the orphanage, I felt even worse. And George, meanwhile, had stood up to Mana on my behalf, had defended my right not to wear a bra, had said, "Does she really need one?" and moved his arm toward my chest, even though he thought I shouldn't fuss about it—and he was right—and when she made me leave, he hadn't considered staying on without me, not for a moment. He'd packed up and left with me without a word. And he'd been so gentle with the children, he could sit and play quiet games with them, or loud ones. He seemed to slip into any situation with ease, had such simple good looks, a humble manner, and he had his wide silences when he would retreat into himself and I couldn't share where he was, couldn't even ask him about it. This also seemed admirable to me, since I had no silent space inside me where he couldn't be.

Once, back at the university, we had had to go to court and had been sentenced to community service, a string of Saturdays pulling weeds for obstructing a government vehicle. The crime had been an elaborate joke on our part, layers of jokes, private references to characters in books that had led to us lying down in front of a parking ticket truck and refusing to get up. But no one else got the joke—driver, police, judge. It was always like that with us. In my dorm we'd talk to people in a nonsense language and think we were hilarious. We wrote secret messages on the blackboards of the physics tower classrooms, our version of graffiti. We liked to think we were different, special, bonded.

Pulling weeds was harder than it looked, though. The roots went deep, and if you got only the tops they would grow right back. I know we pulled at least one weed.

The truth is I had (have) a dread of being left.

The year before all this, when I was seventeen and still in high school, my family had left Chicago and moved to the Southwest. The plan was for my mother and little sister to stay with me until I finished high school, but they kept going away for visits that seemed to grow longer and longer. Finally the day I graduated from high school my parents sold the house, drove away in a moving truck, left me alone in Chicago. It was just for a few weeks. I was scheduled to spend a month in a school program in Spain. My grandmother offered to take me in, but I refused, not because I didn't love her but because I felt angry with the family for more or less leaving me behind. It wasn't the first time something like this had happened. And it wasn't the second time either. The fact is I'd been sent off or left behind, ignored, many times over the years. They'd always been that way with me.

I'm not saying I was a deprived child. My family was tirelessly middle-class. I'd been raised in the city, grew up riding around on the train, ate peas and spaghetti for dinner. When I was thirteen, we moved to a house in the suburbs for the high school. I was shuttled around in a station wagon. I saw the advent of MTV. Still, they did ignore me.

When my parents moved away, I told them I would stay with friends. The situation made my friends' parents uncomfortable, I guess. Three different sets of parents, parents of my very best friends I'd had for years, told me I was welcome to stay at their house for one night but then I had to leave. Miriam's mother said I had to leave first thing in the morning. I don't know if they all consulted about this or if they independently decided they didn't want me. I wasn't a great kid. I'd done some drugs, I'd stayed out late. I didn't have many run-ins with the law. I didn't talk back to non-parentals. I didn't skip school all that much. I was a pretty regular not-great kid.

The final night I was welcome at a friend's, I couldn't sleep. The family all went to bed and I sat on a stool in the kitchen. I listened to my Walkman and felt angry and abandoned. I sang songs to myself about leaving it all behind, about not needing anybody. I wanted to be harder. I was working at it, working at being harder, at not caring, talking myself into it. It's the first time I can remember determining to be a certain way, setting out to be a certain type of person.

The next morning my friend drove me to our high school. We'd both graduated the week before. I went in the front door and walked down to the basement. I propped opened one of the basement windows with a small rock. That night I came back, crawled through the damp bushes, and dropped in the window with my bag. I slept in the gym on a pile of mats. The school felt huge around me. The gym was cavernous, three standard-sized gyms connected, one end spotlit over by the badminton net, a chair stack of silver parallel lines, and the rest of the space—the other gyms and the empty spectator seats—spread out in a smooth sea of darkness.

The second night I dropped down into the basement from the window and came face-to-face with a janitor.

"What do you think you're doing?" he said.

I didn't know what to say. "This is my school."

He pointed at me with his broom. "This is *my* school," he said.

"My parents left."

"Oh." We considered this between us. Also between us: his broom, four squares of tile, a few years, maybe more. He lowered the broom. I lowered my bag. "You can visit anytime you like," he said. He took the rock I had used to prop open the window and he broke the lock with it. I appreciated that.

I was thinking about all this while George and I sat on the ground, waiting for a bus to take us to the city, the wait looking like it could be a very long time. I was thinking about how George hadn't left me, hadn't threatened to, how he'd come after me in the hills, even though I'd been wrong and had deserved to be left. That seemed like a supreme loyalty now. I lifted my head. Conditions, I told him, had changed. And I needed to let him know. The situation, I explained, had come to a point where I could no longer not say that I loved him. I just loved him and there was nothing I could do about it and I was sorry about that. And then I pulled part of my dress over my head. (I used to do that.) And he said, "Come out of there" (he used to say that), and tugged at my dress until I came out. And then he said, "You are the nicest person I've ever known," and then he said, "We should get married," and I said, "Yes, we should," and then he said we should get up because he thought a bus was coming, and indeed, as we got to our feet, we could hear it roaring up a hill.

George liked to sing. He used to speak the words more than sing them, shout them. I did whatever he did, so I shouted the words too. We stood on the road and shouted them together.

You can get anything you want at Alice's restaurant.

VISITORS

Once we left the orphanage I more or less had a bad attitude from there on out. I didn't want any more guns in my face. I didn't want any more Marshall Law. There was some confusion on this point. Before we went to Central America, George had told me that San Salvador, the capital of El Salvador, was under martial law. He said it several times and it comforted me every time because I thought he was saying Marshall Law and that it referred to a restructuring program that I messily confused in my mind with World War II and the Marshall Plan. Imagine my surprise when we arrived. We got off the bus in San Salvador in the middle of the night and a squad of soldiers came sidling over, clanking with artillery like cowboys.

"Hey," they wanted to know, "what are you two doing, standing out on the street like this, violating curfew?"

Excuse us?

"Everybody has to be in by dark," they said, "and here you are, milling around outside with your bags. Let's see your papers."

The other people from the bus got into taxis and cars. I recall the red taillights going down the street and then George and me there alone with the soldiers.

George spoke mediocre Spanish. Later he spoke it so well that he developed a slight accent in English and couldn't shut the

Spanish faucet off even when he wanted to. Spanish just came out with the English. Meanwhile I spoke it beautifully, but later less and less, until today it sounds fake, like seeing glowing stickers instead of stars. But at that point George was having trouble understanding, and I myself couldn't get my head around this curfew business. It felt like a new language, one that I knew but somehow the meanings of the words had been switched on me. The only curfew I knew of was the one my parents had imposed in high school. For an entire city to have to be in by dark was too strange for me. Around us was a city of iron-vault streets, thousands of hearts beating in the walls.

The soldiers searched our bags. They told us not to be out after dark again and they were not nice about it. They put us into a taxi.

"We'd like to go to a hostel, please," said George.

That sounded good to me. We had been in hostels in Guatemala and Mexico, and that's where I wanted to be just then—among our kind. I wanted a set of good old-fashioned gringo heads lit up in front of me. I wanted to see that tourist smile wiped on a face.

The taximan frowned into the rearview. "Hostel?"

"A cheap hotel. Where the people are like us."

"What are you like?"

"We're from another country," George explained. "We carry backpacks."

The man turned around and took a good look at us. Then he drove us to a brothel and left us there.

We spent a lot of time in that brothel over the next few weeks. We sat on the landing outside our room. The ladies did their washing in the courtyard below. The sky was gray all the time over that building. The place seemed muted of color. We leaned our backs against the wall, stretched our legs out across the walkway. When the ladies came up the steps with their visitors, we got to our feet to let them by. They just stepped over us if we fell asleep. They didn't speak to us or even look at us, or even look at each other. (This was specific to El Salvador. Later we stayed in a brothel in Honduras, where there were only insurrections, not a civil war, and the ladies were so friendly, they came into our room and told us stories all day and even robbed us, twice.)

I don't know where they got these prostitutes, but they didn't look like any I'd ever seen and even at my age I'd seen a few, and anyway I knew what one was supposed to look like. These prostitutes wore blouses and knee-length skirts. They had neatly combed hair. They looked like the kind of ladies who work as clerks in business offices, or like airline ticket agents or case workers at a social service agency. They looked like the kind of women who type your number into a computer and make you wait a long time and then tell you in a voice at the edge of impatience that they're sorry, there's nothing they can do. You'll have to come back tomorrow. Just to look at them made you feel a Kafkaesque hopelessness.

We sat on that landing because our room was depressing—peeling walls, stained sheet—and because it was awkward to be out on the streets. Men with enormous M-16s stopped us every few blocks and wanted to see our papers and ask us just where did we think we were going and what were we doing in El Salvador. George wanted to go out anyway. I didn't and I wasn't going to let him go without me. He had to talk me into coming along. From here on out, in fact, George had to cajole me into doing anything. We argued endlessly about this, first in apologetic tones, later in harsher ones. "What is the point in being here," George would say, "if all we do is sit in our room?"

"What is it out there you want to see?" I said. "Buildings we could look at in books?"

"We need to find people to interview."

"We don't have to go out for that," I said.

People filed in to see us. Somehow they knew we were there. I was mystified by it, but it occurs to me now that obviously George knew we were being watched, but he didn't want to frighten me. One man turned up and said he wanted to see our room. I have no idea who this guy was. He was nice-looking in his suit. He looked like a movie star. He was shaking our hands and making jokes and walking back and forth across the room, waving. He stood over our backpacks and pulled our clothing out of them. "*¿Qué es ésto?*"

"Ha ha!" he screamed. "Can you tell me what this is?"

"What a weirdo," I said to George.

"I think he's searching us," George said in English. "I think this is a search."

"That," George told the man, "is shampoo. You put it in your hair. *Y éso es un zapato*, yes."

"What are you doing here?" the man said. He had a fistful of tampons in his hand and behind him the window to our room had bars. I stayed quiet.

"Visiting," said George.

"What for?"

"Tourism."

"Oh yeah? What do you want to see?"

"*Playa*, beach."

"*Playa*'s not here. *Playa*'s over there." He pointed with his chin.

"Ruins, then. *Las ruinas*."

"*¿Arruinada?* Ruined what? There's nothing ruined here. Only ruined thing is in here." He thumped his chest, then reached over and, with the back of his hand, thumped George's chest.

Another day another man showed up. He had one of the ladies with him. They walked up the steps, passed us, and then stopped. The man turned to us with a bow. He was heavyset, unshaven, but light on his feet, a head of curly hair. "*Desculpe*, do you guys know how badly things are going in this country?"

We nodded. We'd heard that.

The lady looked away.

"The government is bad *¿sabes?*" He went on and on. People are poor, dying off, missing. He knew what they were saying in the States, he said, that El Salvador was a democracy, but it wasn't true. (He was right about that—now everyone knows the truth about the death squads in El Salvador, but at that time in the States there was a lot of talk about El Salvador, the stronghold of democracy in the Communist wasteland of Central America.) He said he didn't know what we were doing there and he said he wasn't going to ask. He said he may be in trouble even now for coming to talk to us, but he wanted us to know that the FMLN could make El Salvador better. He was very eloquent. "I don't know what you're doing here," he kept saying. (Salvadorans always want to know what you're doing in their country, even if you're Salvadoran. It's the great national question. I never know what to say. Why wouldn't I want to see their country? So many people want to see *mine*.) George and I were too scared to answer. We thought he might be an actual revolutionary and after what we'd seen—the paro, the orphanage, the curfew, clear sincere danger—we weren't sure we still wanted to sign up. We said nothing.

Then he said, "Don't remember me." He repeated it, sternly. "Remember this country, these people, but not me." He took the lady's arm and led her around us, back down the steps, and he never came back. But it's hard not to remember a man who orders you not to remember him. There is a similar mind exercise involving an elephant.

BROKEN CITY

San Salvador was cleared out, hardly anyone on the streets except for all the different kinds of militia. People were staying indoors or had gone away or "disappeared" or were dead. Plus an earthquake had knocked down half the city the year before and the government still hadn't sent anyone around to pick it all up. Concrete walls lay in apocalyptic pieces on the roads. People were living in the rubble in plywood houses they'd put together, tin tops tied down with strips of plastic. In places it was hard to get through. Cars shifted around the piles. George talked me out of our room each day and we walked all over that broken city, looking for people to interview. We went to the Casa Presidencial over and over and were never let in. We waited at the gate and argued with the guards. Behind them the Casa looked like a compound behind the barbed wire and fences. It seemed far away, a distant white fortress, colonial-style. George and I found only four people in El Salvador willing to talk to us on tape. One was an artist. He wore a fine blue suit and was friendly and calm, having his soda from a straw, but what he said shocked us, and later we said his words again and again to each other, we couldn't stop saying them, but I don't remember what they were. (And of course the tapes are gone.)

We went to churches, to the cathedral. No one would talk to

us. The cathedral was ravaged, birds flying in and out the broken windows, bare rebar coming out of the walls. The story went that years earlier, before the civil war, a new cathedral had been going up, a better cathedral, tremendous, full of paintings and glass and statues on platforms, like a birdcage full of color and light, and El Salvador was to have a new archbishop, Oscar Romero, sworn in too. But no sooner had he fit on his robes than he said enough was enough. The government was gunning down all their priests, and he'd had it. If they thought they could stick this robe on him and he'd just sit and smile, well, they had another thing coming. The church officials could not understand why he said that. The government killed one little priest (a friend of Romero's, yes, but still), and suddenly the guy went berserk. Romero had been a conservative his whole life and now he became a raving radical, ranting about Vatican Two. Who knew he had rebellion sleeping within that aging body? All it took was one priest downed, and the end of the yarn was tugged, his entire soul unraveled.

Oh come on, said Romero. No one would believe the number of priests killed in El Salvador. It's like a horror film the way they were being plucked one by one off the countryside, tortured or shot, the bishops writing sadder and sadder letters to the president, "Stop killing us please." And on top of that, said Romero, here the church was spending God knows how much money on a new cathedral when anyone could see the hungry people sitting outside, sleeping on the steps, which clearly runs against the teachings of Vatican Two. Romero ordered the construction of the cathedral to stop and for the money to be given to the poor. (These liberation theologians and their Vatican Two.)

The cathedral was three-quarters built when Romero told the workers to stop. The workers just left. The building began to decay. People brought flowers. People brought umbrellas to pray in the rain. Romero talked on the radio and all of El Salvador listened. He talked about government persecution, he demanded an apology, a pasture of apologies, he demanded a new order. In 1980 Romero was gunned down in the middle of mass and the Salvadoran Civil War began.

By 1987 a film of graffiti had settled over the city, over the benches and walls, the statues, the steps, the roads, the trees, cars, and fountains. It all read the same:

EL PUEBLO EXIGE LA RENUNCIA DEL PRESIDENTE DUARTE

MUERE REAGAN

DUARTE ASESINO DE MÁS DE 70 MIL SALVADOREÑOS

FUERA DUARTE, OLIGARCAS Y YANKEES

YANKEE GO HOME

We played hangman in a notebook, George and I, when bored in our room. He made words up, didn't play by the rules. "That's not a word," I'd say.

"How do you know what's a word?" he'd say.

One day we took a bus to the coastal resort town La Libertad. We'd read in our guidebook that the finest beaches were in El Salvador and that all the surfers of New Zealand lived but to get there and ride the Salvadoran waves. We got off the bus and walked down to the ocean. But the water was brown. It was streaked with black lines in both directions as far as we could see. What the hell? My suit itched under my dress. We walked on the beach, poked at black clumps of seaweed with our shoes. We were the only people around. We walked back up the sand. We asked a man in a hotel why it looked like that. He took us upstairs. We looked down at the water. You could see the heavy streaks across the water, running out into the sea. The man told us the water wasn't really brown. It looked like that because of algae. It would be gone soon, we should wait a few days, he said.

I'd never seen the Pacific Ocean look like that.

It must be a terrible war to make the water look like that, I thought.

I looked over at George. I wondered if I should be marrying someone who took me to places like this.

We couldn't have been very high, looking down on the beach, maybe one or two floors up, but in my memory it seems as if we were very high and I could see a long way.

WONDERFUL TIME

In fact I'd been to El Salvador. When I was six years old, my mother and father took the whole family on a vacation car trip to El Salvador. We drove from Chicago to San Salvador in a station wagon, stopping in Mexico to see my grandmother. We slept in a tent. This was in 1975, just before the trouble started.

I remember driving down the gravel road through the rain forest. I remember the station wagon breaking down over and over (though my mother says it was a Dodge Dart and that it broke down only once), and I remember my brother and me playing in the mud. We took a tiny airplane someplace and then we saw some buildings (my mother says that must have been in Guatemala at Tikal), and then a Native American slept with us in our tent (she says that was a hired guide), and I peed in my sleeping bag. I listened to *Sesame Street* on my tape recorder and then a bad man cut my chin with a knife (my mother says this last one didn't happen). Then we got stuck in a traffic jam and I was sick with a stomachache and I had to hold my head out the window so I could vomit onto the road (my mother says that didn't happen either, or if it did, it was in Mexico City or Texas). I remember the car kept breaking down. Dad was angry all the time and yelling. I wanted to go home.

My mother says it was an adventure. She says we met so many nice people. She says we all had a wonderful time.

GOOD IDEAS

Afternoons on the landing at the brothel I closed my eyes and prayed. What did I pray about? I prayed that everyone on Earth would get what they want. But then I'd think about that and decide that was an awful lot. People want so much. So I prayed for people to get these particular things that I named in my mind, or at least for these particular people that I named to get these particular things—or for them to get them when the time was right or when God wanted them to have them, if He did. If God didn't want them to have the things they wanted, then I didn't want them to have them either, and it was probably wrong to want them, so I prayed for their souls instead.

I prayed for us to not want what we want but to want what He wants, whatever that was. How was I supposed to know what He wanted? I'd never even prayed before that year. I prayed to learn what He wanted somehow—not to have the knowledge of God and the hubris that would come with it, but to see dimly the plan or at least the section of the plan that involved me and the people I knew so that I could pray for the right thing.

Or at least, I prayed, let me pray for the right thing accidentally, by coincidence or mistake.

I was reading the Bible that year. The Sermon on the Mount with its revolutionary spirit, Ecclesiastes with its gloomy complaints. George and I read together, taking turns reading aloud. We read books about theology. We read the ontological and teleological arguments for the existence of God—Saint Anselm, William Paley. We read Kierkegaard and Lessing on human striving. We argued with Hume. We read books on Christology. We talked to the liberation theologians and copied their expressions: "The preferential option for the poor"—does anyone remember that one? Or "institutionalized violence"? Some people must remember these outdated phrases. I recall them all. It was my first specialized vocabulary. I'll never forget it. I'll die dreaming of "applying a Marxist analysis to a God-centered system."

My faith also had the side benefit of sending my Jewish atheist family into fits of despair. In my house, Judaism referred to an abbreviated Passover and a few jokes about candles around Christmas. Once I announced I was a Christian, my family whipped themselves into shape. They joined a temple and went every week. They enrolled my sister in Hebrew school. They celebrated holidays they didn't like or exactly understand, found the menorah in the garage. They put up a mezuzah, and my mother joined a Jewish study group for women. They made my sister have a traditional bat mitzvah, complete with a great-grandmother's locket and chairs in the air. By that time I had backslid into my atheist upbringing, but they weren't taking any chances.

Yes, those days of faith were fun for the whole family but, bit by bit after the trip, I walked across the dance floor and sat back down with my family, where I remain, like a wallflower, patting my hair, watching the waltzers, admiring the grace of some, the awkwardness of others, but no, I will sit this one out.

Long after I stopped being a Christian and it was clear my brother and sister weren't going to become Christians either, my mother and father went to temple less and less, and finally they left off altogether, and everybody forgot about it. Except my sister. She is the last to forget. She still can't forgive me for Hebrew school. "Three days a week I had to go. While everyone else was having fun. One day you and your God will pay."

ENGAGED

I found it odd that George wanted to get married.

He'd asked me to marry him on the road to the capital and I'd said yes, so that meant we were engaged now. In the brothel we talked about it, about how our marriage was going to be based on God. We prayed to God and asked if our marriage was okay with Him. And since we didn't hear back exactly, we decided it was okay. We told Him that He shouldn't worry because He was the base of our marriage.

"We're sure not the base," we said. "You're the base, God."

One reason to get married was so that we could have sex. We (he) didn't believe in sex before marriage. This, although we had a very sexual relationship. We simulated sex until climax every day, often more than once, in our underwear. This did not seem strange to me. I'd had plenty of sex in high school. Too much. Anyone who has had an eighteen-year-old boyfriend knows what it is to be sick of sex. I was happy to "wait" with George, as long as it meant we could still take off (almost) all our clothes and have lots of (almost) sex. Except at some point you do want the real thing.

"Now that we're engaged," I told George, as he got on top of me and scooted up my dress, "we can have sex. Being engaged is the same as being married."

"It's not the same," said George. He left my undies on.

Still, he had surprised me by bringing up marriage. I was crazy in love with the guy, but eighteen seemed a little young to be getting married, didn't it? He said that depended. We knew we would always love each other—that's what I had said, right? So what was the difference if I was eighteen or thirty-eight? I wanted to trust him. He certainly knew better around any subject than I did. "Relax," he said. It made me nervous that I was nervous.

He wanted to buy a ring. You would think the ring would be my idea, but it was his. His zeal was of that order. We found the jewelry district in the guidebook, a small block off the plaza, downtown San Salvador, a few dented shops shut up like they were closed except for the signs outside that said OPEN. We walked from shop to shop. The National Guard on the sidewalk kept asking to see our papers. We'd shown them our papers, but they wanted to see them again. The shop owners waited in the doorways and watched, did not call to us, did not smile or prop open their doors and wave us inside. We were the only customers. It must have made those shop owners awfully shaky to have two gringos in there. They must have thought we were spies and wondered for which side. They pulled out boxes of rings and let us fool around with them. I made a big show of being choosy. George made a big show of being patient. I made a big show of being happy. The owners and the soldiers watched. We came away with a little ring for a hundred dollars. It had a tiny diamond and two specks of ruby.

Under an awning, out of the way of witnesses, George put it

on my finger. "For you to wear every day for the rest of your life," he said.

He said we should tell our families.

Another reason to get married was so that his family would be my family—every day for the rest of my life. His mother would be my mother. I wished his mother were my mother and I already pretended like she was. She was George's mother after all and I wanted to be close to anything that had George on it. I suppose she was fairly normal for someone who sounded a bit like a crazy person when she spoke, but I'd never known anyone like her before—calm, undemanding, weirdly religious. She listened to what her sons said and approved. She was a Southern belle, faded, blond, washed out but still beautiful, like a doll left out all fall. I daydreamed about saving her from catastrophes, carrying her up from the depths to the surface, traveling to China and bringing her gifts in small ornamented boxes. I wanted her to know we would be married, that I would be her daughter. "I always wanted a daughter," she told me once. I was ready to be the one.

George called home first. There was no e-mail in 1987, no iPhones or gchat. In those days you could run away and it meant something, by God. You could receive letters from home through the *lista de correos*—an improbable system that somehow worked, whereby the sender would write your name on the envelope and the name of the country you expected to be in, and two months later you'd get off the bus, walk into the post office in the capital, and ask if you had any mail. Or you could call home by going to a phone office, standing in line, and then waiting while they rang up your mother to see if she would pay for the call. You had to pay a small fee either way but you'd have to have a pretty mean mom to say no to a child calling from the middle of a civil war.

George let me go with him into the booth and share the phone receiver. I always did that when he called his mother and I would get hysterical if I couldn't hear her voice.

She was pleased, naturally, that we were getting married. I say "naturally" because that's just how she was all the time: pleased. I never met a nicer woman in my life. She thought maybe we would be getting married in El Salvador.

"No," I said.

"Nicaragua then?"

"Maybe," said George. He looked at me.

Then it was my turn. I sat in the booth and didn't invite George in. I closed the glass door between us.

I didn't want to tell my family. I was scared. I was even a little embarrassed. To say I was going to join the revolution, that was one thing. That could mean anything. That showed I'd kept my sense of humor, even if I had gone mad. But to get married, that was really to put a lid on the thing and shovel dirt over it. I didn't know why I felt that way and I was confused and sad. What was wrong with me?

You ask my mother and father what it was like for them when I ran away to join the revolution and they'll say they were traumatized. But to hear them tell it they were already traumatized. They have a whole list: there was my Christian conversion and, before that, my high school boyfriend, there was my brother from the time he was born, my father's not being able to play baseball, the teasing my mother took as a kid. Still, it's kind of a wonder that they didn't hire a bounty hunter to come find me and drag me home. In fact they didn't do much to get me back. They settled on one plan and stuck to it, and it did finally work: if they sent no money, we'd run out and eventually have to come home. A convenient plan for them, thinking about it now. A nonplan, really, a plan of inaction, of least resistance.

Later, from Nicaragua, I called and invited them to come "visit the revolution," and they said no. Maybe in those days that's simply how parenting worked.

This call went like all our calls, like all our interaction for as long as I could remember. It seemed to me that my father was standing behind a door and each time I opened it he was shouting, so I'd slam it shut and open it a few weeks later, and he'd be shouting again. Was he shouting all the time behind the door? Or did he start the shouting just as I opened it? On this call he said I was irresponsible and intellectually lazy. "Your problem is you don't *think*," he said. Fair enough, but no different from anything he'd said *before* I'd run off to the revolution. Meanwhile, my mother tried to give me a few updates from home: My sister was taking an avalanche of lessons. Something significant was happening to the bathroom. I wasn't close to my family. I didn't know them and I did everything I could to keep them from knowing me. But still, oddly, when I heard their voices coming over the line, I felt a sudden tug toward them, a little insurrection inside me. Despite everything, I felt allied with them. A deep sense of belonging. I looked at George outside the booth, sitting on the bench. He seemed like a different creature from us. I wondered if he had been born wanting to get married. If he would have proposed to a plant.

I didn't tell them about the engagement. I hung up. We began walking back to the room.

"So what did they say?"

"About what?"

"Our getting married."

I hunched my shoulders. "Not much."

"Not much?" He stopped.

"I didn't tell them," I admitted.

"Oh."

In that moment I recalled in a slap-to-the-forehead kind of way what, in my amnesia love-fog, I'd forgotten: I was never going to get married. My mother had once told me not to. She'd said: "Never get married," and it had cemented in my mind. The one piece of advice that made sense.

As a matter of fact, I don't think my mother ever said that. I don't recall her saying it and I can't imagine her saying it. It may have been my mother's sister who said it—my aunt, who'd had a divorce that had seemed to go on for years, so long that I'd believed she'd had many divorces, a new one each year around Christmas. Or it's possible that no one said it. I just heard it without anyone having said it and then it became part of my lore. Who knows how I heard it or why I believed it? All my life, it turns out, the girls I knew dreamed of wedding dresses, cakes, honeymoons, and babies, and I didn't know they did, because I didn't. I assumed they agreed with me, and it was only later that I realized my mistake, when one by one my girlfriends began marrying off, pulling out children, pushing their stuff into houses, while I looked on, askance.

But I loved George and he certainly wasn't offering me anything like the usual girl's gray dream, Simon Says, and so on. But what was he offering?

In that moment, standing on the street—and I can still see myself there, in a loose pink *Flashdance* shirt and some kind of worn skirt, almost curfew time and the day dimming along the edges—I saw suddenly that this was all a game for me. The Christianity, the running away, the marrying. I was going along with it, but I didn't mean it, and I didn't like it. I didn't like the orphanage, the soldiers, the brothel. In fact I hated it. It hit me like a chair over the head. I hated not eating enough, hated my dirty clothes, hated San Salvador, hated George in some way because he'd brought me here and because I knew he meant all of it.

But I loved him too, for the very reason that he did mean it, all of it, he was someone who *could* mean it. I'd never known anyone like that. I wanted to be with him. I wanted to *be him*. I couldn't be away from him.

Still, the thought that I'd have to live this way, the way we were living, always, that I'd be married to him and my world would forever be that small, as small as the biggest the two of us could make it, and that there would be nothing else that couldn't come from the two of us, that was hard to swallow. Suddenly how big we could make it looked pretty small and that was too big to get down my throat, that smallness. That wasn't going to fit.

Not everything is explainable by something else. You can love something and be afraid of it. You can want someone and want to run away from wanting them.

A big contradiction was standing in my face and I knew it, and now, waiting beside me, he knew it, and he was going to let it stand there and so was I.

"Let's go back. I'll call them again," I said.

"It's too late. Forget it."

"No, I'll call them."

"No."

I pulled his arm. "Come on, we're going back."

I didn't know then that there is a different smallness. Your world is small in a different way if you don't share it, if you don't wrestle with that struggle of you and him, and how to make it big enough for both of you to fit.

This time he squeezed into the booth with me. My mother accepted the charges.

"Great news, Mom," I told her. "I forgot to tell you. I'm getting married."

My mother said, "Now how is that great news?"

PARADE

There was the day in San Salvador that we went to the plaza. It was more or less deserted except for the police forces, the military, and the *guardia nacional*. We spotted a few citizens moving through. I hadn't wanted to come and now that there was so little to see, I hoped that meant we could leave. "You see?" I said to George. "Nothing here." Suddenly we heard drums, the regular beat of western drumming, and a parade came marching along. No one saw it, except us and the soldiers and a thin line of locals who obligatorily assembled. In my memory it seems as if the parade was going by a few inches from my nose, so large I could see only hands, faces, drums, the white and red uniforms, the sway of the legs of the stilt walkers and the purple material of their costumes, their eyes through the masks. They stopped in the middle of the plaza. The drummers played a marching tune. The clowns and stilt walkers waved and teetered around. Then they all went on.

HEAVEN

The man was very sure that we could build heaven on Earth, that that was part of the plan. Do houses pop up ready-made? No, free houses do not fall out of the sky like Dorothy and the dog. You construct the thing yourself if you want to live in it.

George and I were at "la UCA." It has a nice sound. La-*oo*ka. The University of Central America in San Salvador. I believe we were interviewing the Jesuit priest and liberation theologian Padre Ignacio Ellacuría. A poster of peasants hung on the wall.

"You make the world that will be eternal," he said.

This was doctrine liberation theology. I, for one, felt God could have been more clear on this point from the start. Heaven was like taking the airplane to Spain, was how I'd learned it. You land and come out into a world of moorish buildings and sunshine, familiarish language. Someone came along and made the place, thought it up. All I had to do was appear and it was mine.

The priest began talking about the United States, and I stopped listening. I knew what he was going to say, and what was I going to do about it? I accept the blame. On behalf of my country I apologize. Some drawings sat beside the desk. The priest saw me looking at them. "Oh, a local artist." He lifted the drawings. People lying naked, side by side, handcuffed, whip and burn marks on their backs, legs, necks. He held one up to the wall. "What do you think? We thought we might hang them."

I honestly don't know why these people agreed to talk to us.

George had the questions. Is capitalism evil. Does God condone violence. What is the role of the church.

A couple of years later, a few meters from where we sat, Father Ellacuría was shot in the head.

A couple of years later, in November 1989, the leftist FMLN guerrillas, in an attempt to usher in the kingdom a little faster, came into San Salvador and took over large parts of the city. It was the biggest and greatest thing they'd ever done. Unfortunately no one in the whole world cared because with typical, incredible, Salvadoran bad luck they'd launched their attack the very same week that the Berlin Wall came down. The guerrillas entered San Salvador only hours after the first sledgehammer hit the Wall. Across the ocean the East Germans were stepping over the rubble, walking into the West. Of course the Wall falling was only the latest, most dramatic sign that the world was about to change, that the Cold War was ending, and for Central America, it would mean the rapid crush of the revolution, but for that one week the army couldn't bomb the guerrillas out, and the FMLN was the image of itself it had always meant to be, even if no one was watching.

On November 16 at one in the morning a group of Salvadoran soldiers of an elite U.S. Army–trained battalion marched into la UCA, pulled six Jesuit priests (liberation theologians to a man, insurgent sympathizers, Ellacuría among them) from their beds, arranged them in the grass, and one by one shot them in the head.

Back in 1987, Ellacuría pushed back from his desk and said our time was up.

CLEAN

Years later I returned to El Salvador alone and I went around the country. It was 2001, and they were finally painting Romero's cathedral. Scaffolds were set up and men were walking all over them, putting angels and sky on the walls, filling in the empty white spaces. I met a man who told me about that crazy November in 1989, the month the FMLN captured the city and the priests at la UCA were shot. He'd been a high school student in San Salvador at the time. The FMLN had come into his neighborhood and entered his house.

"They wanted food," he told me. "My mother cooked them a big meal, meal after meal. You can't imagine how well they ate. They slept lined up on the floor. One morning I looked out the window and a huge tank stood in front of our house. It took up the whole street. So the FMLN ran away and the army moved in. They put a missile launcher in the window and my mother dusted it every day. 'Mom,' I said, 'stop dusting that thing. It doesn't matter if it's dusty.' Still, she dusted. And she tidied. All day she went around the living room, putting the grenades into little rows and folding the soldiers' clothing. They never lived anywhere so clean."

PART THREE

INTERNACIONALISTA

SARAH'S

George and I had gotten nowhere with joining any revolution. It was August. We'd been fired from one job and hadn't found another. We'd managed to throw up a wall between us or at least some small obfuscating stones (a dot of diamond, two glints of red). And now we had to get out of El Salvador. Our visas were running out. We couldn't wait around for people to figure out what they were going to do about the bridges that had been exploded on the road to the border—put them back up, explode somebody back, chart a little path through the river—no time for any of that, George said, because to be stuck in El Salvador with an expired visa was no joke. So we set out. We rode under a tarp in the back of a truck with some guys bringing black-market gym shoes to Nicaragua. The truck drove in loops, searching for bridges still standing. A few kilometers from the border, the guys threw their duffel bags off the truck and jumped out, ran into the trees.

At Salvadoran customs we had the deepest, longest search of them all. The soldiers spent hours scratching our money with their fingernails and going page by page through our books. We were so bored by searches by now, had had so many, we didn't care what the soldiers did. We sat on a curb and watched.

At last we arrived in Managua, the capital of Nicaragua. We

pulled into the station. I was aggrieved, begrimed, laden. I'd had exactly no fun in months and I was ready to blame George for it. I filed to the front of the bus and looked out over the heads of the people waiting to get on. And there, amid the chaos of the station, I spotted a North American. He had two cameras around his neck and stood a foot taller than the Nicaraguan people around him. I hadn't seen any other North Americans since Guatemala. He seemed so tall and white and bald and fat, I was stunned for a moment. My first Internacionalista.

He raised his finger and pointed at me over the crowd. "Hey, you!" he called. "You can't be older than fourteen. What are you doing here?"

"I'm eighteen, you old dog," I yelled back and stepped off the bus into the revolution.

Compared to El Salvador, Nicaragua was like Ping-Pong. The two countries were nothing alike. El Salvador was your basic mail-order military dictatorship: terror and torture, stuttering civilians. Nicaragua was more like a cheerful Communist kazoo concert. Nicaragua had once been like El Salvador. A line of Nicaraguan dictators, the evil Somozas—a father and two sons—had had their hand on the country since 1937. Then in 1979 the revolutionary Sandinistas had come down from the mountains and into the capital and run the Somozas out. The Somoza family fled on airplanes, lifting whatever they could and throwing it into the cockpit. The Sandinistas marched into the National Palace and installed themselves. Nicaragua became a socialist country, the only one in the hemisphere other than Cuba. It was a big capitalist scandal and the United States was enraged. But the Soviets loved it, sent supplies and weapons and men, and bragged about it on the radio.

In El Salvador there hadn't been anyone like George and me. We'd been alone, going around on the streets. In Nicaragua there were hundreds of us, thousands, so many we had a special name: we were called Internacionalistas, and we came from all over the world—Europe, Africa, all the Americas. We had professors and scientists among our ranks, and farmers and newspapermen and a brigade of artists, all trooping around, looking for ways to help the revolution. We converged on the capital and trucked out to the towns, to Granada, León, Estelí, carrying every kind of equipment—hoes and seeds and cisterns and books. We were ready to scrape up whatever was there and pat down a nice new revolutionary one instead. Joining the Sandinistas was like joining the Peace Corps, the Peace Corps with guns. We held poetry readings and story time. We did tricks for the kids. We looked for air-conditioning. We would make this revolution, we swore. Our team would win.

Since I was the youngest and spoke Spanish, the Internacionalistas could tell me to do anything and I would. Every day there was something for George and me to do. On Thursdays we went to the U.S. embassy to protest U.S. support of the Contras, the reactionary group trying to take down the Sandinistas. (Their very name annoyed us: Contra-Revolución—who would want to be against the revolution?) A hundred Internacionalistas or more showed up each week at the embassy gates and waved signs and shouted. Priests gave talks in front of the line of military guards. Buses pulled up and dancers hopped out, and musicians and tightrope walkers and mimes. They clowned, sang ballads of corporate evil, pantomimed Contra destruction. We put down our signs so we could clap. I never saw anyone go in or out of the

embassy (there may have been another door?), but we marched in
our circles and chanted.

The fact is George and I were very good at chanting. We did
our share everywhere we went. In Guatemala we had gone to protests and chanted along heartily. The chants in Spanish were easy
and rhymed: *¡Pueblo, escucha! ¡Tu hijo está en la lucha!* The
Mayan chants were much harder. Even the ones that had been
translated into Spanish were a paragraph long and included
images of flying people and growing plants. Each Mayan chant
ended with a cry against the landowner, a thank-you to friends, a
prayer to the corn and the sun and a long list of saints. George
and I started out bravely along with them but couldn't keep up.
We were mumbling and shuffling by the end.

On Sunday afternoons we went to *la misa campesina*, peasant
mass, where Uriel Molina, a great priest of the revolution, talked
about what God had revealed at Vatican Two, the new directive,
"*Lucharemos o moriremos!*" We will fight or we will die! he told
the Internacionalistas, because the place was always full of
Internacionalistas, so many that buses had to bring them. They
filled the church, sat on the floor, stood in the back, blocked the
campesino murals. Some had to wait outside. There was hardly
room for the Nicaraguans. A few Nicaraguans, the musicians, fit.
They played their instruments on the side. Some Internacionalistas danced, marimba-style, in the aisle. Some took photos of the
walls.

"Where are the Nicaraguans?" George said. "They're missing all
the fun."

"Oh, they come in the morning," the Internacionalistas said.

"Imagine," said George, "what it must be like in the morning,
when the Nicaraguans are here, if it's like this now."

One week George and I went to the Sunday morning service.

We woke very early and rode several linking buses across town. The church had Nicaraguans in it, but it was silent. No music, no shouting, just Molina at the front murmuring mass. "You should come at night," a man leaned over a pew to tell us. "The Internacionalistas come at night."

"Why do you come in the morning?"

"The Internacionalistas are asleep," he said. "A church is not a place for dancing and making fun."

Managua heat was mean and the Internacionalistas had to share the fans. Sometimes it became too much and we would split up and go hunting for air-conditioning. The one place we knew we could always go was the Hotel Intercontinental. This was a strange-looking building, constructed like a concrete staircase to the sky. We called it "el Inter," and knew it as the hotel where the real journalists stayed—not the screwups with rock music and a tape recorder—all the famous people from New York and Washington who wanted to see the Sandinistas. It was the only place in town that never ran out of food, that hung on through the revolution to its old-style waitstaff (nothing is worse for the service industry than socialism), that was rumored to have a rooftop pool, sparkling sun chairs around it in a star (though none of us had seen it). Yes, el Inter was capitalism incarnate. We used it as shorthand for all that was wrong and greedy in the world. We secretly wanted it and felt guilty for it.

In '72 Howard Hughes had been living up on the eighth floor of el Inter in the months before the great earthquake, the one that took down the whole city, but left el Inter standing. All the top military brass used to go there, smirk over drinks at the bar. There'd been machine-gun battles fought in the lobby. There'd been assassinations. The rebel Chamorro had once shot a rocket from one of its windows at the most evil Somoza of them all, the second son.

Later Somoza himself moved in, crouched through the barricade days before he fled the country. In 1979 Daniel Ortega stayed in those rooms in the dawn of the new order. Jimmy Carter slept on the eighth floor while taking in the Communist sights—and when George and I arrived a year later, the bellboys were still talking about it.

The Internacionalistas used to go to el Inter to cool off. It was an easy walk from the cluster of hostels, and any old Internacionalista could go over and sit in the lobby as long as you made a show of looking in the gift shop and being animated and didn't stay too long or fall asleep. Then the security guards got to know you and shooed you out. George and I were eventually barred.

Every night at six o'clock the Internacionalistas went to Comedor Sarah. All over Nicaragua there were food shortages, water shortages, shortages of all kinds: cars, clothes, paper. If you showed up at Sarah's at seven the food was gone. If you showed up at eight the beer was gone. Anyone who showed up at eight had to sit in the back and drink a disgusting red cola called Rojita. We sat on benches and talked about the revolution. Ben Linder, Oliver North, city zoning, the bridges blown in Jalapa. We talked about God and the economy. South Africa, the French Revolution, Trotsky and Marx. We sang the Internationale in different languages (*Völker, hört die Signale, auf zum letzten Gefecht . . .*). George, who back at school had been incapable of a regular conversation, here could sit and talk all night. The Internacionalistas liked George and me, except for the Christian part. They said that all the time. "Except for that Christianity crap, you're all right!" I took this as a compliment. George, though, you didn't want to start on that one with him, boy.

"Fuck God. Who cares about that stupid myth," someone

would say, and George would be off arguing with him for hours.

Later back in our room at the hostel I'd say, "People don't like us if you talk about it all the time. You don't have to talk about us being Christians all the time."

"I don't," he said.

"It comes up somehow."

"They bring it up."

"*You* bring it up," I said.

"No, *you* bring it up," he said.

I denied it, but he was right. I couldn't help myself. "I'm Debbie and that's George," I'd say. "We're Christians." The people around us could say who they were in three words and be fascinating. Christianity was our single distinctive trait.

One week Comedor Sarah was full of jugglers. A group of jugglers had come from Canada. They'd gone to the northern mountains of Nicaragua, to the war zone. "We walked from town to town," one told me, "juggling."

Imagine. We were walking across their war, juggling. We were bringing guitars, plays adapted from Gogol, elephants wearing tasseled hats. I saw it myself and even then I found it a bit odd. The Nicaraguans wanted land, literacy, a decent doctor. We wanted a nice sing-a-long and a ballet. We weren't a revolution. We were an armed circus.

At night the Internacionalistas would go back to the hostels and sit in the atrium and drink Flor de Caña rum (except George and me, who tried not to drink, being Christians). They'd get into arguments, call each other capitalists or fascists, shout, and bang the tables. Then they all became friends again and sang revolution songs until two or three in the morning. They left the atrium like exiting a stage, calling to each other, waving and blowing kisses, holding hands.

The cast shifted each day. Some left to work in the north or headed off to a different town. New Internacionalistas arrived. Some days Sarah's was so crowded, you couldn't find a seat. Other days it was empty and when you came in, looked for faces, you'd find only one table occupied, two compañeros huddled over a map, a lone German in a corner sewing a button, and even if you didn't particularly like the Internacionalistas—their racket, their mess, the very space they took up with their long limbs—still, the loneliness set in without them.

SANDALISTA

Years later I heard that the Sandinistas referred to us as Sandalistas, not Internacionalistas. We wore Birkenstocks, right? A bunch of hippies, ha ha. I don't recall hearing that during the revolution, only after. I believe the Nicaraguans called us Sandalistas behind our backs.

That's okay. I can take (or be) a joke.

In fact I did wear sandals. I brought on the trip my smartest pair, not Birkenstocks, but a strappy affair. It turned out the revolution was going to involve a lot of walking. A week into Mexico my feet were blistered and my sandals were broken. I bought a new pair for five dollars and I wore those until they broke too. I bought another pair and another. Finally George said I couldn't keep buying new pairs. I had to make the pair I had last. At that point I had a pair that cost about three dollars. The sandals stretched after a few days and fell off my feet as I walked. I took some string and tied them to my feet. When the string broke, I tied knots in it and tied my sandals back on and kept walking until the soles wore through to the ground. Why didn't I bring a pair of damn Birkenstocks? I thought. But I'd wanted to look nice, you know, cute for the revolution.

CHART DAY

One day George and I took a bus out of the capital. We wanted to see a breezy little town. It was north of Managua, somewhere in the mountains, and we'd heard it was the place for fun—tiny sandwiches, music outside. We'd heard about a fruit cup. An Internacionalista had described these fruit cups to us, how a Nicaraguan lady served them in her kitchen. We were holding it between us, the idea of it and its possibility, the soothing cool fruit cup.

But when we arrived we couldn't find any fruit cup or any food at all. We hunched around the town. The streets were so cobbled I kept tripping. We walked by clumps of shrubs, boarded-up restaurants, walls painted pastels. It was lonely up there, hardly anyone on the street, no one to interview, the sun taking its long walk down the road.

It could be like that in Nicaragua, empty where it should have been full. You could find spots without a person to be found in places you'd expected a crowd. Blinding streets, troubled wind, suddenly nobody anywhere.

"Where are the freaking fruit cups?" I said. There was nothing going on there. I wanted to head the hell back to Managua.

Then we turned the corner and came on a Nicaraguan fair or a party! A bunch of old friends with giant signs—big charts and graphs on wood panels. We moved in closer and watched the old friends set them up in a line. They called us over and took us on a tour. The charts showed how many Nicaraguan people could read now compared to how many Nicaraguan people used to read. How many doctors they had now compared to how many they had once had. Maps showed where the land was these days and who owned it, compared to who used to own it, and what plants were growing on it, and how these plants were better than what plants used to grow on it. You couldn't turn around without bumping into one of these things. It was like an outdoor art show.

I can still see George in my mind, thumbing the charts, huffing with the Sandinistas. He was happy. Before I met George I'd been so lonely and I felt like he'd saved me, but the truth is George was lonely too. I believe he always had been, all of them were, his whole family. Those brothers looked lost, and the mother and father too, each seemed bewildered in their own way, a family of uncomfortable people, bored, estranged, uncertain. But on the day we saw the charts George was flourishing. The Nicaraguans too, marching around the panels. (They'd been lost too, if you thought about it, during those long Somoza years, a whole nation done in, adrift.) Now on chart day everyone looked dolled up and giddy, strong with the pleasure of self-determination.

Say what you like about the Sandinistas, they were a lot more fun than the other Central American governments, who were frankly just a bunch of crabs.

The Nicaraguans took us into the courtyard and showed us whole rooms full of charts too and also photos of people who could read now and photos of children with shoes on, and giant maps showing all the places where children now wore shoes. Out back people had come and put more charts on big boards and stood them in the fields for the Nicaraguans to look at. The boards were large shapes of color—red and black (*¡El Frente Sandinista!*)—and the people of the town walked among them.

But where were the freaking fruit cups? There were just a lot of charts and maps and graphs in that town.

For the Internacionalista, there were small-sized versions for purchase. Little wooden square pins to bring home to friends. Revolution pens and bookmarks. *¡No pasarán! ¡Aquí no se rinde nadie!* George and I bought an army of the stuff. A revolution pull-toy for my little cousin. A revolution book of poetry for my grandmother. A revolution hairpin for my sister.

FEMINISM

George and I were having an argument. We were going to inter-view Ernesto Cardenal, a liberation theologian and the minister of culture, a top man in the government of Nicaragua. We had spent all week preparing. The guy had written several small poetry books and we read them in the original Spanish. We took notes and discussed what we might want to talk to him about. He was a priest and had lived on an island in the middle of a dark, shark-infested lake until the revolution had come along and taken him away. He had written repeatedly and vividly about how his only wish was to end world poverty and greed once and for all so he could go back to the shark-infested lake and stop it with all this government nonsense for which he'd already been scolded once by the pope. George wondered if Ernesto Cardenal wasn't being a little disingenuous about wanting to quit the revolution—who would want to leave? I, for one, believed Ernesto Cardenal and thought he was brave.

But that was not the argument.

When we did interviews, George asked all the questions. He wrote them down in a notebook beforehand and read them off the page. We did it that way because he had a plan to write his senior thesis about liberation theology—that was what the inter-views were supposed to be for—but I did all the interviews with him and I helped him think up questions and by the time we got to Nicaragua I was wondering why I didn't get to ask questions as well.

It was in Nicaragua that I began to be aware of things like that. I don't know why—maybe because we were engaged and I was afraid we were going to have to get married, or maybe because Nicaragua itself prompted such awakenings. It's true that in Nicaragua I saw women soldiers for the first time. I met women traveling alone from all over the world, women who carried knives. I'd been harassed by men clear down the coast, men grabbing my breasts, men touching me on buses. Men asked to buy me from George. Once, I was alone in our room and a man broke in, and I had to scream and cry and punch to get him out. A soldier chased me through a field once with his thing out of his pants in his hand (that's how I described it to George: his "thing"). I never got used to it or had any sense of humor about it. I was angry all the time, sometimes a low simmer, sometimes enraged. It was unfair that men didn't have to put up with this treatment but could dish it out whenever they liked.

I said that this time I would like to ask some questions.

"You don't know how to ask questions," George said. "If you want to ask questions, fine, but you should practice on someone less important."

"I would like to ask some," I said.

"Why don't you ask one question," he said.

We went to the interview. We waited for Ernesto Cardenal in a small white room. At last he came in. A short man in loose white clothing, a white beard, and a black beret, like a Santa for the liberation. He sat down at the desk and waited for our questions. George began.

Even I could see the questions were no good, now that we were right in front of him. Ernesto Cardenal had been asked questions like these a thousand times. When is violence justified? Again with this question, we could tell he was thinking.

"Well, is that all the questions?" he said finally, rising. He was polite, but he had better things to do than answer these questions again from these two, what were they, teenagers? Who let them in here, anyway?

"Wait, I have a question," I said.

"All right," he said, turning back. "What is it?"

I asked my question and even as it was leaving my mouth ("Tell us the truth, do you or do you not want to go back to that shark lake?") I knew it was not a good question either. He answered it nicely and he left.

Later we united in our defense: How were we supposed to come up with good questions when everybody else had already asked him all the questions? That guy talked to everybody, which showed a thing or two about him, if you thought about it. And he certainly put on airs in that beret getup. We could have used something big to happen around there just then so we could have asked him about it. An earthquake. Then we would have been the first to ask him: "Padre Cardenal, what do you think about the earthquake?"

So we were together against Cardenal that day, but really it was me against anyone who didn't let me ask questions.

DOCTORS

When the Sandinistas took over the country, they handed out medical degrees and set up clinics in every town. Anyone who needed a doctor could go—free for the Nicaraguan, five dollars for the Internacionalista. George and I went all the time. We started out the trip pretty healthy but we got sicker and sicker. Each time we got sick, we didn't get entirely better so we grew a little more sick and a little more, and finally we just stayed sick. We were sick for months. Diarrhea, nausea, stomach cramps, lethargy. George lost twenty-five pounds, and my stomach slowly expanded, became weirdly bloated, smooth and balloon-like. It was in Nicaragua that being sick became a serious bother. The first time we went to the clinic we saw separate doctors. The doctor I saw took me into his office, had me take off all my clothes. Then he put his hands on my butt and my breasts. "Are you sexually active?" he said. "With how many men have you had sexual relations? Describe your first sexual experience." I came out of the office and was shaking for hours. After that George and I went to the doctor only as a team. The second doctor treated us together. He saw us together and gave us the same medication and we took the pills together and threw them up at the same time. The third doctor we saw gave us the same medication again and needles to shoot ourselves up with and vials of a liquid that would keep us from throwing up. We couldn't figure out how to use the needles and George tossed it all in the trash.

After that we didn't go back to the doctors for a while.

We also met doctors in hostels or at Comedor Sarah or on tops of ruins—Cuban doctors, German doctors, doctors from anywhere you could think of. We heard advice from them all. You could buy medication over the counter anywhere in Central America. We started getting whatever pills people recommended as long as they were cheap. We tried many different medications. We took antibiotics for months, switching kinds each week, sick through it all. Sometimes the diarrhea turned into straining diarrhea, where you shit water but had to work at it as if you were constipated; sometimes it became bloody diarrhea, which we hid from each other because we thought there had to be something really wrong with that and we were afraid; or we had diarrhea plus fever, which may have been the worst because "fever" didn't mean a temperature of a hundred and one. It meant skyrocket fever, a hundred and six, and it came out of nowhere, had an onset time of minutes, and could knock you to the floor anywhere you were, leave you unable to move, unable to form thoughts, unable to fear death. The first time it happened was to George on a bus, a seven-hour ride. I was hysterical, weeping and begging people to help. I was certain he would die and leave me there with his stiffening body. I was furious at him for doing this to me—and how on earth was I going to tell his mother?

One time I had an incredible number of bites. You could barely see them, but they itched like mad. George kept saying, "Wow, you are a mess. Look at you," because I couldn't stop scratching. George said he didn't want to sleep next to me because the bites might spread over to him.

"Bites don't spread," I said.

"They do on you," he said, and he was right. They'd spread to my fingers and between my fingers and then to my arms, my stomach, my legs, my ankles. I had to keep stopping on the street, so I could sit and scratch.

Then a Nicaraguan lady told us, "Those aren't bites. Those are bugs living under your skin and when you scratch, you spread them."

We thought this was helpful. This was progress and it made sense (though it was gross). We tried to get rid of them. We tried to freeze them to death by holding ice to the bites. It didn't work. An Internacionalista suggested we suffocate them with chewing gum, that we put the chewed gum on my body, covering up the bugs, so the area would be sealed off and they would die. We discussed it. Would gum work? Or would the sugar in the gum feed the bugs? Did the bugs even need air? Was there air in the gum that would seep through and onto my skin? We bought gum, an enormous quantity of gum, and we tried it.

There is something wrong with this picture: Where did we get all the gum from? There were rations and shortages. Often we did not have enough to eat. How did we find gum? Well, we did. I can't explain it. Somehow the gum was there and we sat around and chewed it and stuck pieces of it to my body. We had to chew it well, and I had many spots that needed it. We asked some Internacionalistas sitting in the atrium to help. We sat around chewing and sticking pieces of gum to me, between my fingers, on my stomach. "How long should I wait?" I said. We didn't know. First we thought twenty minutes, but then we thought maybe thirty. Then George said wouldn't it be a shame if we took it off and they were almost dead but not quite dead. All in all I think we waited about an hour and twenty minutes and then took it off and it didn't work. For weeks it went on and we didn't know what to do. I was desperate, I was in despair. It was a crisis.

Then suddenly I got sick of the bugs or forgot about them, or the bugs forgot about me and left or died, and we all went on to something else. They went away. I don't know how.

Many things are like that.

Another time a doctor from Canada was alarmed by what we ate. We ate whatever we could find, we ate from venders on the street when they were there.

"From the venders?" he said. "You cannot eat the food from the venders."

"Well, people eat it," we said. "Someone eats it, we eat it."

"You shouldn't eat it!" he said. "And what are you doing about the mosquitoes?"

We weren't doing anything about the mosquitoes. What were we supposed to do?

He went on like that about all we did wrong. At last he sighed and said, "Can you do the waltz at least?"

Alas, not even that.

"Now, that I can teach you," he said, and he did.

"One two three, one two three, one two three," he said. "Here, put your hand on my shoulder. Good. Now you two try it together."

He clapped and called out the numbers while we danced up and down the landing.

BICICLETAS SÍ, BOMBAS NO

The Internacionalistas signed George and me up to build bikes.

Because of the trade embargo, Nicaragua had fewer and fewer cars and trucks. Buses looked like cartoons of buses with too many people on them. Cars were dropping parts along the road, were held together with paper clips and pins. The Nicaraguans would ride bikes, the Internacionalistas decided. A company in China donated five thousand unassembled bicycles and sent them over on a boat. George and I were going to assemble them.

We reported to the mechanic the first morning, a bikeman from some rainy state in the U.S. North. He said he would teach us what to do. He was very good at teaching and serious about it. He used many words and hand gestures. I was so busy watching him teach me how to put on an electrical unit that I forgot to listen to what he said. Finally he stopped and handed me one of the electrical units.

"Give it a try," he said.

I gave it a try.

Later we didn't know what to do about how angry at us he was getting. He kept looking at what we were doing and then saying, "Honest to God!" and grabbing the electrical unit and putting it on like he told us to before. George knew a little about bicycles, had ridden one as a kid, could change a quick-release tire, blow it up with air, but he seemed only able to hold the tools or walk across the room holding them, which infuriated the mechanic. The mechanic had three Nicaraguans working there, real pros who could wrap a chain in ninety seconds, and another Internacionalista, a pretty blonde, Sammy from South Africa, who was funny and wise. I began following her around the shop, imitating her accent and the way she walked. She was thirty-seven years old and as soon as I met her, I hoped to be thirty-seven one day.

"George," the mechanic kept saying, "hold this."

"Why should George hold that?" Sammy said. She had a habit of raking her fingers through her hair. "Can't I perfectly well hold that?"

"Yeah," I said, pulling at my hair. "I can perfectly well hold that."

I remember the day the mechanic asked Sammy to sweep the shop. She was on about that all afternoon. "The woman sweeps the shop, yeah? Of course! You ask *me* to sweep!"

"I cannot *believe* this," I said.

The day the mechanic fired us—all the Internacionalistas—waved his arm at us and told us to leave, we slumped out, never to return. The three of us, George and Sammy and I, walked over to Comedor Sarah. We got beers all around and sat outside under the wet trees. We were men out of work, George and Sammy and me. Fired by the revolution. We sat around telling stories of other revolutions we'd known. In El Salvador. In South Africa. We made fun of the mechanic—the guy was asking for it.

"Honest to God!" we said.

"The bikeman looks out on civilization," we said, and made solemn faces.

It was one of the best nights of the trip, the night the mechanic fired us. We got a coveted table—half outside and half inside—and it wasn't even raining. The night air buzzed with cicadas and the moisture sat low in the sky. Normally it was just George and some random Internacionalistas I worried were going to take George away from me. But that night I felt like one of the gang.

Suddenly dinner was ready and it was coming out on plastic plates, fish raised high and passed down rows over the tables (no menu at Sarah's, just one dish for everyone—"This is socialism, after all," we said), a single eye fried and up on the plate, fins and skin caked with some rusty substance, cartilage protruding. The Internacionalistas began singing, everyone taking turns with their home country's national anthem, Sammy waving her fork.

We stayed late that night, me sitting beside Sammy. The cicadas were so loud I couldn't hear my own "s" sound when I spoke. My "s"'s were the same pitch as the sound of the insects, so my "s" sound was drowned out. Sammy talked about apartheid and Nelson Mandela: "The desire to stop apartheid is really a desire for socialism," she said. "It has *nothing* to do with racism." She told me about her job as a schoolteacher, about her walk to school. She talked about lost love, all the men she'd left, and how the love she'd had for these men didn't seem lost anymore, it seemed cast off, discarded and forgotten, which I thought was tragic—to have loved and then to have no longer loved. She shrugged. "I have other things in my life."

It was the first time I could imagine myself without George. I could see a new me looking out through the glass back at myself sitting at Sarah's, a woman watching a girl who was looking back at the woman—no man, no boyfriend—each just absorbed in her own contemplation of the other. I felt nostalgic for what I'd lost (cast off, discarded), though nothing yet was gone. And when the rain finally came that night, even it seemed miraculous, that where I'd just sat was now wet. We waited under the awning at the edge of the rain and darkness.

"I was a mess at your age," Sammy said, reflectively. "I never could have come here the way you have."

Wait, I wasn't a mess?

NERVOUS

It's hard to explain how nervous I was. Later George always talked about how we'd been "running around those countries," as though it'd been fun. Mostly I did not have fun. I was nervous all the time, not so much of the danger, although there was that, but more, I was nervous that either we were going to have to get married or that George was going to leave me. I could hold both of those in my mind at once. I could be beside myself. Marrying was bad enough, but what would I have done if he had disappeared or fallen in love with someone else? I depended on him for everything. I didn't know how to take care of myself—changing money, finding bus stations, I was right beside him all the time. I adopted every belief he had. I repeated it, garbling it somewhat, like a parrot. I reproduced a higher-pitched version of it. I looked at everything through his eyes. I wanted to see what he saw. I didn't want to see whatever I saw. I didn't know what to see when I looked. I worried all the time that someone would take George away from me—maybe even Sammy, who cares if George was only twenty-one? They were both wonderful, it made sense they'd want to be together and leave me behind. I had to become friends with her and stay near her as much as I could so she wouldn't run away with George and so that she would feel guilty if she even thought about it. And I had to stay near George too, of course, which meant I had to have both of them near me at once. The three of us wound up spending huge amounts of time together, which only made me more nervous. I pined for San Salvador, where I'd had George to myself. In Nicaragua everyone was a threat—citizen, soldier, Internacionalista. I kept a careful eye on him.

It occurs to me now: How did I not drive him away?

It was exhausting being nervous. I looked forward to the day I wouldn't have to be afraid.

As for him, it wasn't his fault that he had to do everything for me or I would fall apart. He didn't seem to mind my dragging around after him. He kept his independent spirit. He helped me, hurried me, included me in his tedious, endless political and theological debates. "She makes a point," he'd say, then resay whatever I'd said so it made sense. He'd sit squinting at an Internacionalista interlocutor—the squint that let me know they didn't have a chance. George would nod, listen, squint madly, until the Internacionalista wound down and quieted. Then with a few easy steps he'd take their argument to pieces. Sometimes people would never speak to us again after George was through with them. A Mormon once packed his things and left town in the middle of the night. An atheist once became violent, kicked George, who yelped in surprise like a puppy.

George grew sullen sometimes, and this could last for days. He'd barely speak, sit alone, sink deep into himself. He'd ignore me. He may have been reacting to me: I was beginning to have small fits of rebellion. Or maybe he just needed a break from my neediness.

"What's wrong?" I'd say, following him down the street. Maybe he was sick of me following him everywhere?

"Are you mad at me?" I'd whisper to him at a protest.

"I'm trying to listen here," he'd say, lifting his chin.

Maybe he didn't like me anymore?

Or worse, maybe it had nothing to do with me at all.

Once we showed up in a town with no hotels, George and I and some Internacionalistas—a scientist lady, a man from Canada, a woman from Austria. We were standing in the street, holding our belongings in our arms, not sure where to put them down. At last a Nicaraguan family left their window and came out of their house.

"All right, all right, you guys can stay with us," they said. "But get out of the street, for Christ's sake. Do you want to get run over by a *burro*? Ha ha."

It was just one big room up there, where the family put us, and this was upsetting because I was certain George was going to run away with one of the Internacionalistas, even though they were all in their thirties and very unimpressed with George and me. And George was upset because who should the scientist turn out to be but another big fat feminist, just what George needed. The feminists seemed to do nothing but order me not to listen to George, order me not to stay with George, not to marry George— I told everyone we met that we were getting married. The scientist Internacionalista thought our engagement was a hoot and said that if George wanted a doll to play with, she'd give him a Barbie.

"Come sit here," she said to me and patted the bed, "and let me tell you the story of soccer. I invented it, in fact, when I was eleven. In my school the boys played football and the girls played hopscotch. I wanted a game we could all play together, so I made up soccer."

"You did not invent soccer," called George from the other side of the room.

"Yes, someone else invented it before I did," she said. "But I didn't know it, had never seen it. So technically I invented it too. As a way we could all play together."

"That isn't how we use the word 'invent,'" George called.

That afternoon the feminist scientist kept walking around the room naked. Both of the Internacionalista women did. I was amazed.

"Wow," I said. "That's pretty neat the way you walk around like that."

"Who cares how I walk?" said the scientist. "You could walk around like this all day and we'd be bored to tears."

I took my dress off and walked around in my underwear. She was right. No one seemed particularly interested, not even George, who was dehydrated and flattened to the bed. He wasn't feeling well and had diarrhea. My coming-of-age story, if I had one, would be right here. It didn't involve a loss of innocence or man's inhumanity to man. It was me taking my clothes off and marching in a circle around the room. Somehow I knew—nothing specific, I just *knew*—I wasn't who I would be. More of me was coming. It doesn't seem like much, but there it is. The slow shift in the tectonic plate of my soul began. I wouldn't always need him. I put my dress back on before going out.

MORE OR LESS, 2001

Many years after I pulled my dress over my head and knew there was more, I didn't feel like there was more. It was 2001, and maybe there was even less. I had my dress over my head again and my swimsuit on. I was looking down at my body. The same size but older. I was on a tourist beach in Panama, sitting on a hotel patio among the kinged and queened Europeans: the Norwegians, the Belgians, the Brits. They were gathered on the patio, running up from the beach, shaking sand out of their hair, settling down to drinks and backgammon. They all looked like George. He used to wear a kind of pants that later became popular for tourists. I kept catching glimpses of the pants and I always thought it was George. Everywhere I looked I saw ghosts of him that lasted for half a second and then were gone.

The Europeans were speaking broken English, as they do when an American arrives, because of course (they assume) no American knows any language but their own. "This holiday," said one. "I walk in mud to the beach and get sunburn and sand flies and ants to attack to my feet. I in mud walk back. This holiday is harder than work."

"This holiday," said another, "I could have building a ship and sailing away on the money I spend on rum and cigarettes this week."

I stirred my drink with Panama's plain flag on a stick. "I had a holiday once," I said. "Not far from here, during the revolution in Nicaragua."

The Europeans paused, turned to me.

"The country was full of guns. There were soldiers all over the streets," I said. "Fourteen-year-old boys with grenades."

A standing European took a seat. No one else moved.

"There were food shortages, war," I said. "Old-line Soviets walking around."

I may have been laying it on a bit thick.

"I worked for the Sandinistas." Well, I sort of did.

"And in Managua," I told them, "you could drink the water from the faucet."

"*Aso?*" The Europeans' eyebrows went up. Hey, this was too much. From the faucet?

I nodded. "They filled the water with chlorine."

A European raised his drink. "Now that's an adventure."

"Oh, not so much." I smiled. "Tell me one of yours," I said, wickedly—for who in this crowd could beat me?

The Europeans looked at each other. "Raccoons attacked to our tent one night, but it's not much to compare."

PART FOUR

SICK OF THE REVOLUTION

TIRESOME

The Internacionalistas were so happy. Nineteen eighty-seven was the year we romped in the sun and played in the streets. The Nicaraguans loved us. We all laughed at each other's jokes even when we didn't understand them.

But sometimes the revolution became tiresome for the Internacionalistas. Managua was tiresome. Every day the restaurants and stores ran out of food. The rice had rocks in it and we all chipped our teeth. No one had air-conditioning and we had to share the fans.

Of course it wasn't as tiresome for us as it was for the Nicaraguans. The Internacionalistas were a hell of a lot happier about the revolution than the Nicaraguans. We could go home anytime we liked. The Nicaraguans were stuck. "Nineteen eighty-seven? Ah, yes," a Nicaraguan will tell you, "that's the year we had no toothpaste. We brushed our teeth with salt. We had no—what is the word?—*jabón*, soap. We washed our clothes with the seed of a tree."

But the rocks in the rice, the shortage of water, that was nothing compared to the war, the draft, year after year, all their young men dying off or running away, no one getting any richer, promises sinking like stones. The revolution was a pain in the ass, if we wanted to know the truth. And on top of that there were also all these tiresome Internacionalistas around, who expected much and became disappointed.

The Internacionalistas, well, we knew we could be tiresome. It wasn't our fault we were tiresome. We were just standing there, not doing anything, not wanting to be tiresome, and there we were, tiresome.

The Nicaraguans felt the same way. They were just standing around in their own country, in their own *town*, and here come these Internacionalistas, calling it tiresome. Hey, Sandalista, we didn't ask you to be here. Whose revolution is this anyway? Freeloaders is what you are. Why don't you stay in your room if you're going to go around with a face like that?

So after George and I held signs at the embassy protests, after we spent our Sundays at the church, after the bikeman gave us the boot, after we'd been in Nicaragua a month or more, I got dysentery and did stay in our room. It was around then that things took a turn for the worse.

I lay on our bed and came out only to use the bathroom. The bed was made of giant rubber bands stretched across a frame. A burlap sack covered the rubber bands and the sheet was pulled over that. The burlap rubbed through to your skin. The pillow was heavy and hard, stuffed with sawdust. The heat was like a fist. I was dizzy, bored, depressed. I lay on the bed, irritated with George, irritated with Nicaragua, irritated with God, who was getting pretty tiresome Himself. I listened to the Internacionalistas talk outside our room all day. They never stopped talking about the revolution. Did they have nothing else to talk about? Was it the only thing that had ever happened on the Earth? You could tell what kind of Internacionalista you were dealing with by their similes. "This sure's not like Detroit!" they said. I stared at the ceiling, could think of no reason for the comparison. It was a syllogism. A is not not-A: This sure's not like Iran! Nobody drops and prays to the call of the muezzin. At least it was more logical than the ones who said, "This is exactly like India!"

Then I got dehydrated and vomited thin strings of bile.

Then I just stood over the toilet gagging.

"This revolution is a drag," I said. I didn't say, "I want to go home."

BLACK MARKET

Then George started trading dollars on the black market.

"Oh, yes," I said. "Fine. Mr. Moral. With his principles."

First he'd told me we wouldn't trade on the black market. If there was one thing tearing apart the revolution, he'd said, it was corruption—bribes, black market, crime. "We'll play fair," he'd said, "and in this small way we'll be revolutionaries, revolutionaries of the economy."

Well, there isn't anything so revolutionary about obeying the law or, for that matter, breaking it, but fine, good, agreed. We will be revolutionaries by obeying the law, George. No black market. So then what was he doing trading dollars on the black market right here in Managua?

"All right, all right," he said. "We can't all be perfect, can we? Have you seen the markup on the córdoba? It's absurd. If they're going to make it impossible for us, what else are we supposed to do? Are we supposed to starve while everybody else eats?"

Okay, so that one thing. Trade dollars, nothing else. So what was he doing buying food on the black market? Stolen military tins and plastic packets of peanut butter?

"Somebody's going to buy the stuff," he said. "It may as well be us because at least at heart we're trying to help the revolution."

But somebody stole that from the soldiers. The Sandinista soldiers, the good guys.

"Well, it's stolen already. We're not going to find them and give it back. Besides, the soldiers probably sold it. What do they want with the stuff? And these plastic packets travel well. Who knows the next time we'll see peanut butter or the next time we'll be dropped off on some dusty crossroad with nothing to eat? In fact, it's probably stolen from the Contras. No way is this Russian-issue peanut butter. Have you ever seen a Soviet eat peanut butter? This has got to be United States Army issue. Reagan peanut butter. We're taking food from the enemy and putting it in the mouths of the revolutionaries."

Fine, buy black-market food, that one other thing, but nothing else. So what is this, was he actually bribing that clerk?

"Now look, do you know how much it costs to extend our visas? How are we supposed to help this fine revolution if we have to pay all our money just to stay? We were going to spend the extra money inside the country in any case, so what's the difference?"

But bribery? What would God have to say about that? That must be the limit, that must be over the limit.

"Render unto Caesar what is Caesar's, render unto God what is God's. It's easier for a camel to pass through the eye of a needle than a rich man to enter the kingdom, Debbie. Remember Jesus at the moneychangers, turning over the tables. Use your head, Deb."

So bribery, as it turned out, that wasn't the limit. Smuggling, that was the limit. Except that wasn't the limit either. We could do anything. We could steal, we could look into faces and lie, we could forge documents, we could pull tricks and run. It was fine, it was part of the revolution. It was our Christian duty.

TO BLUEFIELDS

George and I set out on the road to Rama. I didn't know why we were going to Rama. I couldn't see any sense in it except that it was the mouth that led to Bluefields, a place he wanted to go— there was the promise of an interview with the leader of the Miskitos, if we could make it, the promise of an interview with the mayor. I couldn't see any sense in that either.

The more resistant I was to whatever he wanted to do, the more determined he became, and, in turn, the more difficult I got. We could be like this about everything.

I'd gotten over the dysentery, but still had diarrhea, and who wants to go on a bus with diarrhea? He said we would hitchhike—an outrageous suggestion. But he said we *had* to, because the buses weren't running or were filled or delayed, and the line to wait for one looked longer than the road to Rama, which was no surprise, I said, since getting anywhere around Nicaragua was always that much of a hassle. So instead of waiting in line or asking around or trying again another day, George had the idea of Rama in his head, that gateway to Bluefields, and the idea of our arriving at its gate, and that was it.

I was fasting. We had developed a theory that the best cure for diarrhea was to starve it out because a woman we met on the street told us that diarrhea is a hungry bug feeding off your plate.

Plus I had a cross around my neck because an Episcopalian gave it to me with some idea that a cross would help. Because God likes crosses. Because God changes fates. Because God loves humans and not the diarrhea. Because God wants people to ask Him for things.

On our first day of hitchhiking we stood at the side of the road at five in the morning with all the Nicaraguans who also thought hitchhiking out of Managua a fine idea, with their baskets and bags and boxes and children. We all stared down the road. Finally a man picked us up and dropped us off in a small town where we waited for hours. I didn't know the name of the town and saw nothing in it I would want, now or ever. Even the ladies in the shop seemed to see their town as what they got in place of what they'd asked for. I sat on my bag and read a book about the plague while George stood in the dust shielding his eyes. He asked everyone who came by for a ride and no one would give us one no matter what. We were that unwanted. The town had no hotels. The trees were leafless and wind-bent. The store sold only Rojita. The sun was like an illness.

"Would you come over here and help me?" George said. "Stop reading that dumb book?"

"No," I said. "I will not."

Finally George gave in and we got a bus that came by. It was going as far as Santo Tomas. We rode like pebbles in a can on those roads. In Santo Tomas we waited again for hours to get a ride. How many hours are there in a day even? But George was determined to get to Rama. We sat outside and waited. The road stood before us and ran behind us like a thing denied and another discarded. The sun was like another language. The sun was like a shout in the sky. The sun was like the landscape. The sun was alive, like an animal. It was a dull knife. It was a clock, a tunnel, an eye. The sun was a year long. It was like breathing. It was official. It rocked back and forth like a lamp.

Then the people of the town said, "You can't go on, the soldiers are putting up a barricade." And indeed they did. Big blocks of cement and wood dragged into the road and spikes set up all over it in case someone thought to drive in a truck and push the blocks away. And they posted soldiers on the road and around it out in the fields, watching in both directions in case some poor sap came by on one of those Chinese bicycles. Everyone gathered around and watched the proceedings and said over and over, shaking their heads, "You'll never get to Rama tonight. Never, never, never."

But George held out hope a little longer. "Maybe a tank will come by and take us."

"A tank, ha, that's a laugh," they said. "What do you think this is—El Salvador?"

"A tank," they said to each other. "He thinks a tank is going to drive in from Honduras and pick him up."

At last he understood that we were not going to make it to Rama that night.

There was only one hotel in the town and it turned out to be the most unbearable hotel of the trip. This hotel room had no fan and it was too hot to close the door and there was no fan and there were spiders outside the room. Who crawled in if they could. And there was no fan.

I have always been afraid of spiders.

The worst of it was this question: door open or shut? I would no sooner decide the door must remain shut when the heat would grow intolerable, like something intending to kill, and then spider infiltration seemed the better option. But the spiders were not mere daddy-weaklings or jumping spots. They were large and hairy. They had balloonish bulges on their backsides. They looked alien and territorial and evil. And there weren't only a few crawling around. There were hundreds, there were thousands. They hung in a system of webs like maps, like constellations. Webs ran up and down the walkway, hung in a heavy net overhead and extended down to the handrail and spread across the walkway over by the toilets. The webs shone silver in the moonlight and turned and shifted as the enemy spiders made their way through the maze. And they had to be poisonous. They couldn't help but be poisonous. They demanded it, foretold it. I had never seen a spider like that and I never have again. Maybe that was all of those spiders in existence, they were gathered in that one spot. The entire species evolved on that hotel walkway, undisturbed by owner or citizen or nature or God as the rest of creation is, as they would have been anywhere else—because who else would put up with such a thing? Who else? I never saw them again and I never looked for them either, and they never looked for me. We've left each other alone ever since and may each species—they and I—live forever apart. May we each always be a fading image in the other's eye, amen.

Don't forget I had diarrhea. I refused to cross the webs and use the toilet. I would not crawl into the bushes in that untamed spot. I couldn't hold it. God help me, I shit in the street.

Nineteen eighty-seven is the year I did nothing. The year I fought in no war, contributed to no cause, didn't get shot, jailed, or injured. George and I lost the tapes with the interviews on them—or at least *I* don't know what became of them. We didn't starve, didn't die, didn't save anyone either. Didn't change anyone's mind for the better, or the worse. Didn't make any civil pronouncements or public promises that we kept (or private ones either). We had absolutely no effect on anything that happened. The only thing that changed as a result of our presence was us.

As for the Sandinistas, they had nothing but trouble ahead. The church had come out against them. They were losing the war against the Contras. The age of the draft was hovering around fourteen. The U.S.S.R. was coming apart. Two years more and the Nicaraguan people would vote the Sandinistas out. The health clinics would shut, the schools close down, the tracks of land handed back (and then caught in ownership confusion for decades). Nicaragua would drain of Internacionalistas, molt its socialist shell and shuttle back in line with all the other small countries with absurd problems that obviously couldn't be solved (but some of us remember).

On the third day of hitchhiking George and I stood on the road and waited for the soldiers to pull the barricade away. Then we caught a lumber truck east, sat in the bed on the logs. We rode out of town under dense clouds and then rain and then clouds and then rain, then clouds, then rain, four times total, and we balanced on the muddy logs, bumped along with all the others going to Rama or wherever else they were going to wind up. It was crowded and miserable and wet.

At last we arrived in Rama.
    How far is it from Managua to Rama, by the way?
    Two hundred and ninety kilometers, one hundred and eighty miles.
    By that time I'd forgotten: George didn't want to go to Rama. It was just a tiny town of rain and people up at dawn. He wanted to go to Bluefields, up the thin river from where Rama watched its back. Of course it turned out that no commercial boats went to

Bluefields anymore because of the war and the things that happen to boats in war. George said we should sit and wait in any case because, well, what do these people know. How do they move cows and such if not on a boat? So we sat, most of the day, down by the docks, and it looked as though it had never not rained. The trees looked as though they would drop their leaves with wet, as though the sun could never hope to fight through the wet. A squat of outhouses over the river, large birds coming through. We waited for a boat. There was no boat, only waiting and rain, rain lifting, then rain coming down again. It grew dark. The small strip of town had no streetlamps. People walked around, leaned against the posts, us too, leaning against the posts, until at last we got a room to wait for dawn. I searched all over that room while George sat on the floor and watched. I took apart the bed and put it back together. I shook the sheets. I didn't find any spiders.

In the bed, in the dark, I said, "Don't touch me. It's too hot."

This is the year I learned how to get a visa. How to pack a backpack, when to catch the night bus. The year I made iodine water for the first time and the year I nearly gave us iodine poisoning. The year I learned where to get a free room, how to save a wet watch. It was the first time I dried clothes on a line, interviewed a politician, the first time I searched for food, the right road, the right bus. First year I cursed at a doctor. This is the year a stranger crawled into our bed in the middle of the night while George was out, the year I hit a stranger over the head with a glass bottle. The first and only year I was an Internacionalista. The first year I was willing to run away with someone, the first year I began to look back, just a bit, became just a teensy bit more disentangled from him each day. The first time I found a revolution, first time I left one, first time I wanted to go home.

I later became an expert at all of these things. Except I never found another revolution, though I've tried.

The next day George and I got a ride out of Rama on a gunboat. It might have been different if it hadn't been for the fact that it rained for ten hours straight and the soldiers kept shouting at us because I was always in the way or for the fact that the river was not the blue and green that a river to Bluefields should be and the trees did not hold out fruit we could pick as we passed, as I had imagined. No, the water was mud, the sky was gray, the trees a tangle on a far shore. There was nothing to eat. The soldiers patrolled every fishing boat, every broken canoe, every patch of thatch clinging to the side of the river. "Anybody in there?" they said, poking with their rifles.

We rode up the river, the rain coming down, a sheet of plastic thrown over us like over a roll of hay. We arrived in Bluefields at last. Beating storm and night. The boat pulled up. A lantern lit the wooden plank to the dock. Not one light shone on shore. A blackout.

"Where can we find a hotel?" George screamed through the storm.

"Hotel? No hotel. The hotels all closed last year. *Por la guerra.*"

We looked down the dark, wet street. We started walking.

CAPITALISM

It had to happen someday: our Nicaraguan visas ran out. Then it had to happen again: our second Nicaraguan visas ran out, and this time the Sandinistas didn't want to give us third visas, since we weren't helping the revolution.

"But we *are* helping the revolution," said George.

"Oh, you're working?" said the official at the customs office.

"Sure we're working."

"All right. Where do you work?"

George looked at me. "Bicicletas Sí, Bombas No," he said.

"Bicicletas Sí, Bombas No?" The official was writing on a form.

"Yes, we work there, we worked there."

"*Trabajábamos*," I said. "Worked."

"Which is it?" He clicked his pen. "You work or worked?"

"Worked," George admitted.

The official put down the pen. "So where do you work now?"

The short of it was we had to leave if we wanted to stay. We had to cross a border and come back—pay the entry tax. George said we should go to Costa Rica and find out why *they* didn't have a revolution. Didn't the Ticos want a revolution too?

Raise your hand if you've been to Costa Rica. How did you like it?

I, for one, will never forget the first hours I spent in Costa

Rica, after being in Nicaragua and El Salvador those months. We rode over the border and from that moment the air was cooler.

"Is the air cooler?" I said.

"Yes, it's cooler," said George. And the road was smoother, George looked handsomer. The flowers were fresher, seemed larger out in the fields. The lines for food at rest stops were shorter, more orderly. The road signs made sense suddenly and people spoke clearly. The bus seemed less likely to break down, now that it was riding away from those ravaged countries to the north.

San Jose, the capital: riding into that city was like riding into Bethlehem or Las Vegas. There was that much holy to look at. Grocery stores and pizza shops, tall buildings made of steel and glass. It was like seeing it all for the first time—that's how foreign it seemed. It was like someone else was seeing it. We felt dirty before it. The city was shining and multiform and complex. We could see out the window of the bus unbroken sidewalks, stores with names, billboards for breath mints, women wearing panty-hose, the faces of TV sets, a line of them on racks, cars on the street less than a decade old. George and I climbed off the bus and walked through the city. We dared to buy things—a can of diet soda, a slice of chocolate cake. We looked in through panes of glass at swimsuits and pie pans and clocks, plastic shaped into toys and containers and telephones (let's face it: plastic was the real revolution). We saw ourselves on the mirrored sides of build-ings. We walked into and out of air-conditioning. We looked at a theater that looked like it had been made to be looked at.

We came to rest on a park bench in the plaza, the city moving in circles around us.

"Capitalism is wonderful," I said, my mouth full of cake.

PARADISE

Costa Ricans are fond of reminding you how peaceful they are. "We are a paradise," they say, and all the tourists repeat it: "This is paradise, we're in paradise, here is paradise." George and I stayed a week in San Jose, looking for interviews, and people told us we were in paradise so many times and with such vigor and pride that we wished they'd say something else. Their primary claim to the title was the fact that the country had no army, which you had to admit was impressive considering the military buildup all around them.

"No army? Ha."

This was an American talking to us.

"Go to Costa Rica, people told me," he said. "It's a paradise."

"That's what they say," we said.

"Come to find out," he said, "I'm the fool. There's police all over the place. Semiautomatic weapons, Mace, clubs. People live behind ten-foot walls here. Every house has guard dogs and barbed wire, electrified fences."

"Yeah," we said.

"If that's not an army, what is? I never saw anything like that in the States."

"It's not like that in the States, true."

I don't know who this man was or what he was there for, but I know it was something dark. People in the hostel had said he was facing charges of treason. That he'd led attacks in the mountains of Nicaragua. Maybe it wasn't true, I couldn't say. He was a thin man. His skin looked sucked in. He wore a light, white Mexican shirt and drank rum from a flask, bared his teeth with each swig.

"I'm getting the hell out of here," he said.

"Go home," I told him.

"That's a laugh," he said.

"People miss you at home," I said.

"That's another laugh."

"Somebody does."

(I hoped people missed me at home.)

"What's home?" he said.

He didn't tell us anything, didn't answer our questions, but I kept watching him, trying to figure it out—what was it about him? And at last I came up with this: he had the scent of defeat on him.

But it was 1987, he should have been in his heyday. And yet you could tell he was already done for. Maybe he knew somehow that these wars were lost and that even the won ones would gain little. Those dusty Nicaraguan shacks would always look the same—through dictatorship, communism, capitalism. Maybe he could see it before the rest of us could.

There were defeated men like this. They started to pop up here and there and then suddenly there were masses of them, not just from the Central American wars, but from Russia, from Germany, women and men, disappointed people, people living a life in the face of failure, not only the failure that we all face—the slow rot of the body—but the failure behind them as well as ahead, the failure of who they'd been and what they'd hoped for. And there was the present failure too, the failure rooted in their being, the failure that entered their dreams.

"We're revolutionaries," we told the man.

"You are tourists," he corrected.

"Revolutionaries," we said. "People call us revolutionaries."

"People call you tourists. Everywhere you go, people say, 'Stop, don't shoot, it's just some tourists.'"

"We only look like tourists."

"In fact you're even dirtier than the tourists," he said. "You should clean yourselves up. The Ticos are tidy. They can't stand you filthy tourists. Not to mention tourists pretending to be revolutionaries. That's the filthiest fucking tourist there is."

He took another swig. Those teeth.

"No offense or anything."

FEVER

Christ, then I got sick again. We were still in Costa Rica. George wanted to head the hell out, get to Panama, see the Noriega dictatorship, and I, of course, did not. We'd made it only as far as the beach, filthy fucking tourists all over, talking about what everyplace else was like except where they happened to be.

"You get flowers like this in Spain," the least amusing Englishman I'd ever met told us. "In India the Coke is much cheaper, five rubles, that's maybe three or four cents, but I bring my own teapot." He had a guy with him, an American, who wore a backpack with a machete strapped to the side. I could hear them and see them in my head long after George and I had gone up to the room to bed.

Our room was at the top of a staircase. At one time the place had been nice, you could tell, but it was decaying in the sea air. The rafters falling down, holes in the floor. The windows had no screens, no panes, just blocks of wood you could fit in or take out for air. An occasional bat flapped in a loop overhead. I had diarrhea and it was getting worse. I woke up in the middle of the night with a cramp in my gut and a pain in my head and the pang of loneliness in a strange land. George was sleeping so hard he looked dead. I crept down the staircase to the toilet and then all the way back up to the room and flopped into the bed with

George, who slept on, dreamlessly I assumed, and when I felt the cramp again, I went all the way down the stairs again and all the way up, over and over. Salsa played from two directions and a rooster crowed wrong all night. The diarrhea went on and on.

It could be much worse, I thought, lowering myself dizzily to the cruddy floor in the bathroom stall with cockroaches crawling down the walls. I could be like those awful tourists without an original thought in my head. I could be holding in my head all those sights and words and prices—a meal in Bombay, the taxi to the airport, the cost of a room in some corner far away where people stop, look, start again. The tedium of it. I curled on my side on the floor. I began to fall asleep, but in the end the size decided it: I couldn't curl properly on the small shit floor in the stall, so I got myself up and began climbing the stairs just as it started to rain.

Oh, of course, I thought, it makes perfect sense that it would be raining right through the rafters and I'd be sitting here (I paused on the stairs, got on my knees), having to go back down to the toilet before I've even gone back up. I kneeled there, gripping the handrail, drops of rain falling on me through the rafters, the mosquitoes buzzing. I couldn't recall if I'd been down yet or up yet and I couldn't remember what the word "yet" meant, something about time sequence, the future or the past? I couldn't get a grasp on it, grasping the handrail, kneeling, the staircase unsteady, as though it might collapse, as though it were collapsing already (is "already" a "yet"?), a slow-motion fall, and it was at that moment, with the stairs and the rain and the rafters, that the fever hit, the kind that blinds, the hurricane kind, the ten-trumpet, twelve-finger kind that whips you off your feet and makes you babble. It was like losing what makes you a human, like becoming a small, furry creature with a fast-beating heart. George must have come wandering out because I remember him carrying me to the room.

Then for twenty-four hours I had no thoughts, could not speak, I was a body, nothing more. George took the towels and soaked them and threw them over my body again and again while I let out gasps of suffering and relief. He tipped my head to drink, pushed pills between my lips, wrung the towels out over my arms and face. The wet, wet towel. I will never forget you, wet towel.

How do I remember all these times and places? It's easy. These were the days I would remember again and again, tell everyone I met, and when I began to write, they were the first stories I wrote down, the first book I wanted to write, the first manuscript I abandoned, and the second, and the third. I have sixteen-year-old drafts of these scenes. Why? What could it matter? A young person goes away and comes home. Everyone has that story to tell. Young people go away for years. A postcard arrives, a picture of water, then nothing. They come back with a small child by the hand, they come back to find no one remembers them, they come back to find everyone dead. They are driven out, they never return. The great works of literature are built on goings and tri-umphant returns. The Bible is full of them—Jesus Himself, we're still waiting, ready to hear what He's got to say for Himself, what elaborate excuse for staying away this long. George and I were nothing. What could possibly be significant about those particu-lar blocks of wood that fit in that window, those particular towels George wet and laid on my head? Why would this trip mean so much that I'd have to keep going back to find it?

It was dawn, the day after the fever, and the light hit my eyes. A pattern of blues and blacks, a slosh of blood or water inside me, a roughness somewhere. My mind began to tick without my per-mission or knowledge, began to form letters, then words, pressed them to the white towel of my brain and left them there to hang—

machete, sun, man, hill—while I knew nothing about myself, did not know whether I was awake or asleep or dead or dying, had arrived at the unconsciousness that all humans fear and long for, but still, despite my virtual absence, the words began to line up, one after the other, and grow into phrases and sentences, all of it directed at the man who seemed to be in there with me, George, who was in there or out there, nearby, and my mind wanted to talk to him.

My mind said, *Tell me, truthfully, George, did you see that guy, he was a tourist, I tell you—some kind of American, I believe—with a machete on his pack?* My brain lit up, turned, ejected its thoughts. *I saw it, George, and I know you did too. There he was, his full pack on and a huge machete strapped to the side of it. Be honest with me: Don't you think it is a bit wacko to go around carrying a machete tied to the side of your pack like a tent?* George was a good companion, loyal, patient. *My point being not that he is going to hurt anybody necessarily, but that he is mad.*

And the strength of the argument, the sheer volume of the voice in my head woke me, degree by degree. Against my will I began to take control of the sentences, direct them, contribute my own ideas, and I wasn't sure if I was speaking aloud, seated on a bus or at a table or what.

Think, George, would you? Think of all the things you could slide into the side of a pack, tuck there on the outside, strap to it. Think of the long, thin things: fence post, pedestal, blueprints, rake, a rama de fuego in flower, a telescope, a tripod, a giraffe (a little one), a brook of water. Why, you could strap a second pack on there if you liked!

Not a teapot. That goes inside.

Being sick was good times between us. That's when I knew I loved him most, when I needed him to pour water on my face.

Why the machete? I asked him in my head, not because I wondered really, but because I liked the sound of the words together like that. And I liked the idea of our answering the question, the two of us puzzling it out. *Why oh why the cruel, sharp machete?*

All the people who have left us, George, I wept in my head, *all the ones who are gone. Mana and Sammy. I can see them, going away across the map, lost, turning around and around. ¿A San José? ¿A León? they call. There's only me and you now. And the music, the sun, the cobblestones, the rum, the night bus, the cock- fights, the cicadas,* el jabón.

It never occurred to me to go home. The only time I even consid- ered it, I didn't consider it. I insert the consideration into my memory because I feel today like it should have been there, but in truth, I remember a time that I *didn't* consider it. I was on the phone with my grandmother. She'd always been nice to me—my grandfather too—quiet and calm, giving me a bowl of sliced fruit. "You're not cut out for this," she said on the phone. "Let me bring you home," as if I were a small ball thrown straight up into the sky. The ball goes up, slows, and for a second it comes to a standstill in the air, torn between acceleration and gravity. There's always the chance that it will keep going up, that the Earth will release its hold at last. Maybe that's why we throw balls?

All I thought in that pause was, Huh? I could go home?

The day after the fever, when my eyes flicked open, consciousness conquering at last, the square of blue beating into the little room, a faded poster half torn from the wall, I wanted to ask him if he could see into me, inside me, the way it seemed like he could, see every thought I had (*Nica libre, Tica linda, bocadita*), and what led to every thought, if he could see each line, each arrow, each staircase and rafter, the small stall of my mind, and even, I wanted to ask him, if he could see how he didn't answer me when I talked

to him in my head, that too was part of it when I woke, the day
streaming in like a stream, a turkey outside making a sound like
a human, a distraught human, wounded, exiled, that too, I
wanted to say and I would say it just like that, "That turkey too,"
but he'd gone out.

WHAT I REMEMBER OF PANAMA

They were our freest days. Or maybe our free-fall days. George and I stopped in Panama from Costa Rica and stayed a week. We weren't trying to join or quit any revolution. We were like true travelers those few days. Just looking, no thanks, don't want any part of overthrowing your evil dictator. Just passing through!

One day we were walking around on the streets of Panama City and we started to notice there were more people than there had been earlier. A little while later there were more. And a little later more. Suddenly there were so many people filling the street that George and I were short on space and getting squeezed. We had to hold on to each other in order not to get pulled apart. We yelled, "What is happening? What can it be?" Everybody was walking in the same direction. We were pulled along with them. The entire country, it seemed, was out on the street. People were hanging from the windows, waving signs and pieces of cloth and shouting things we couldn't understand, and more people were up on the lampposts and more in the trees. "Where are we going?" we shouted to people and they yelled back, but I couldn't clearly hear them. We were carried along with the people, everyone shaking their fists, soldiers all over, armed trucks. I was frightened. It felt like one of those soccer mobs where a sudden stampede starts taking people down. We didn't arrive anywhere.

A little later there were fewer people and then fewer and fewer. Soon there were as many as there had been hours before, and people were walking in different directions. No one was making noise anymore, except one lone man on the corner, calling for his lost dog. Then it got dark and we went to find something to eat.

That was one of the great protests against the military dictator Noriega.

Two years later the U.S. Army landed in Panama, overran whatever was in the way, and swatted that guy into jail.

Later the night of the protest, a Panamanian man began following us. We were in the old part of Panama City, the magnificent run-down buildings left over from when the French tried their hand and failed at the canal. The buildings were breaking into pieces, crumbling onto the streets, and each morning someone came around with a dustpan, swept the buildings up, and threw them away.

"Hey," the man said. "Hey, hello? Are you a Jew? *¿Eres judía?*"

We stopped. I turned around. "What do you want with a Jew, mister?" I said.

"I wish I were a Jew," the man said.

"Oh yeah? Why is that?"

"Jesus was a Jew."

I thought about that. "Peter was a Jew," I said.

"Moses was a Jew," George said.

Stop it, George, I thought. I'm the Jew expert here.

"Was Noah a Jew?" I wondered.

"They were all Jews," the man said. "Place used to be flocked with them."

"Paul was no Jew," said George, a little defensive for his religion.

"But he fell off a horse, you know," I said. "Hit the head."

"And he talked too much," the man said. "Nobody liked him. They were just being polite."

SIXTY BUCKS

We'd been robbed all along, of course, but now it seemed as if robberies and avoiding robberies became the primary activities of our days. We were robbed over and over. We kept our money well distributed among our belongings and on our person so the thieves made off with only a few dollars at a time, but it added up. My parents refused to wire us money and George wouldn't ask his mother. We were eating bread for most of our meals. But still George gave money to anyone who asked, at least a few cents. And he would not be mad if someone robbed us—this was a rule. "They need the money more than us," he'd say. "Blessed are the poor, for they shall inherit the kingdom. Observe the lilies of the field."

I pretended to be pregnant sometimes for free food. My stomach had become permanently bloated. When you looked at me it wasn't noticeable right away, then you saw it, a small swell, and if I had my money belt around my waist on top of the swollen stomach, I really did look pregnant. People would bring food to our room. In one place we stayed, the *dueño* brought me cookies that gave me hives when I ate them but the hives went away in a few hours if I didn't touch them so I kept eating the cookies. He brought them every morning, and I'd swell up and deflate by evening.

Beyond Panama City there was no road, only jungle and swamp you could wade through all the way to South America if you wanted, only you'd probably die before you arrived. I had to talk George out of going. We had no choice but to turn around and go back to Nicaragua only a few weeks after we'd left.

That's when we were robbed by men who never came anywhere near us or our belongings. We were at the border. George was sick. The idea was to hurry into Nicaragua, where the doctors cost five bucks. He couldn't move much, so I had to kind of prop him up while we waited for the bus to leave. I was terrified, as usual. It was my conviction that, as the elder and as the instigator of this whole trip, he should be taking care of me, and if he was lying there shaking with fever, how could he?

He wanted me to buy some black-market córdobas here at the border where they were cheaper. He usually changed the money. I ran off and bought sixty dollars' worth of córdobas from a man standing on the side of the road. The man gave me stacks and stacks of bills—so many I couldn't carry them all. I tried, but they kept falling on the ground and I had to make two trips. I limped back to George with the second batch and dropped them at his feet.

"What is that?" he said, raising his head a little. "What are we going to do with all that? How much did you change, like fifty bucks? Don't tell me you changed fifty bucks. You should have changed ten."

I tried to get the money into our day bags, but it wouldn't fit. I had to get our backpacks down off the top of the bus and shove it in those, but it wasn't going in there either.

"We'll have to throw it away," said George. "Good job."

A lady with a plastic tub of tamales came over. "Hey," she said. "Those guys say they're going to kill you."

"How's that?" said George, squinting at a few men across the street. They were standing in the dust, hands in their pants pockets, looking down the road.

"For the money."

"It's not worth that much," I said.

I could see George thinking, sizing the guys up. Oh come on, I thought, really?

"How about if we give them half," said George at last.

She shrugged.

So we loaded half of the stacks into the plastic tub and watched her cross over to the men. A stack of bills dropped in the dust.

EARLY WRITINGS

The journals are to blame, in part, for the waning of George and me or, more accurately, what I wrote in them. I'm to blame.

George and I both kept journals. We wrote in them, filled them up, and bought new ones. We wound up with a pile of notebooks that we carried from country to country in our backpacks. I don't know how his journals would look to me now, but mine are unbearable, the most god-awful crap anyone has ever written. It causes me physical pain to see them. There are just a lot of prayers in there, declarations about the poor, how I have to help them or someone has to. It goes on and on. I can find a few shadows of the person I was or at least would one day be, but mostly it's a record of my drastic attempts to make sense of Christianity: What does it mean to be three and one at the same time? How can Jesus be fully God and fully man? Is God inside time, experiencing it, or outside of it, creating it? And what is the point in hiding Himself? Why not let Himself be known like a proper king? I was reading the Bible, book by book, which was only confusing me further, with its alien logic, its inoperable moral code, its God with His tantrums. Build an ark, roll the stone. Get out of the way, I'm going to destroy that town. God with His dramatic christenings: You are the chosen one. You are the last born, the tempted one, the one floated away, the thief who will suffer beside me.

I don't recognize the person who wrote those journals. She sounds like she's quoting someone or practicing what she wants to say, lifting phrases from another's tongue—George's, presumably. I get exasperated with her, furious. I want to reach through the murk and shake her, but then another voice steps into my mind and defends her. "She's trying to figure it out," this other me inside me says. "Be patient with her."

We—I and I—stand to one side and regard the girl we were.

George's journals were less hysterical. A mere record of events, which town we went to, whom we met there, what we did after that. "We stopped at the church of Santo Domingo, had a talk with a priest who argued Gutiérrez is right, violence deserves violence." He might add a comment or question: "What would Jesus say?" I know this because I read his journals. I read them all the time, every chance I got. I reread old passages, searching for things I might have missed. I was struck down with guilt over this. I had to wade through my shame in galoshes, but I couldn't stop myself.

I know now that he read my journals too. It never occurred to me at the time, although again and again he found items in them to object to. The journal had fallen on the floor and had somehow opened to this page, he said, and he had seen these four words. He was shuffling around for the repellent and he inadvertently stuck his hand in my notebook and flipped it open and read this sentence.

In the later months my parroting starts to disappear, and there are flashes of irritation with George and then more and more.

"I'm sick of trying to change him."

"I'm becoming convinced that he can be a creep."

"George is weird. I don't know if I want to marry him."

"George isn't talking to me, as usual. Well, it's not as though he doesn't talk to me, it's just that talking to me is suddenly such an effort."

"Should I really marry him?"

"I don't want to be his student anymore."

God was an element too—some days it was me and God against him. Other days it was him and his stupid God over there. I wrote it all down. He read it and grew distant and cold, and I wrote that down too, as more proof, more criticism, and he read that too. He began to develop a caught-bird look, an intensely lonely air, which would stay with him, would become his trademark look for the rest of the time I knew him.

Later, back in the States, the look grew worse. A new kind of reticence fell upon him, less friendly, less playful, as the criticisms arrived not just from me but from a world he'd come back to that he'd outgrown.

Only it wasn't a caught-bird look. That's not right. It was more the look of a caged thing set free. The look of the freed thing the moment it realizes there's a downside.

WATER

We made it back to Nicaragua. Months had gone by since our first visit there. It was that many months closer to the end of the revolution and we didn't know it, but I could feel every day of it, heavy, sitting on the city, though the Sandinistas still had two more years to go. I told George I didn't want to be engaged anymore.

It was a surprise to me that I said it. I didn't know I was going to until the words were coming out of my mouth, "I don't want to be engaged," and as soon as they were out, I realized that this was the only idea I'd had on the whole trip so far, my sole contribution.

We were sitting in our room on the bed. Evening was coming on. I could hear the Internacionalistas in the atrium, fussing toward the door, getting ready to head over to Comedor Sarah.

"All right," he said. He didn't say anything else. I had expected a protest and now I was confused and maybe disappointed. I never knew what to expect from him.

Then I thought we were leaving for dinner. I left the room, but George didn't follow. He shut the door. He locked it.

"Okay," I said. "All right."

I sat on a table in the atrium and waited for him to come out. The Internacionalistas were leaving in groups, ponytailed and radiant. I swung my legs, waited. I was hungry, but I wasn't going to go to Sarah's without him. I never went anywhere without him. If we didn't hurry it up, soon they'd run out of food. Maybe an hour went by, and he didn't come out. I hopped off the table, knocked lightly on the door. "George? Do you want to go eat?" No answer. I could go to Sarah's and see if I could bring dinner back. I'd never seen any take-out containers. The very idea was odd, but you never know.

Then I was out on the street. The Nicaraguan night was having one of its moments, low, white-streaked around the edges. George usually led the way to Comedor Sarah. Which way was it? We were in a new hostel too. All the hostels were only a few blocks apart, a kilometer or so from Comedor Sarah, but I walked and walked and couldn't find it. Soon I seemed to be getting farther, not closer. I tried turning back, but that wasn't right either. I was too far for a shortly strung yo-yo like me. In fact I was lost. I began to panic. I roamed down one street and then another. All the streets looked the same until they started to look different, then very different, and the next thing I knew I was on a long stretch of flat road, fields all around. For all I knew I was walking straight out of Managua. For all I knew I was walking home. The road shone like a river and the sky glowed a hot, dim red. The smell of dung, the unfilled fields. Billboards darkly advertised the revolution. I thought I heard someone call my name. Twice I thought it and both times I turned back to no one.

There was a man walking in front of me. I saw him emerge from the black. He must have heard me at the same moment because he turned, saw me, gestured for me to come over to him, fingers pointing down, meaning: Come here. I stopped (did I know nothing?). He walked over to me. His face was blank. He held out his hand to mine as if to shake it. He mumbled and I couldn't understand him. I leaned in to hear. At the end of his hand, he had bills folded between his fingers. I took a step backward and his other arm swung around and clamped my shoulder like a claw. I screamed and wrenched myself away. He grabbed the back of my dress and I heard it tear. I ran. I drummed down the road. It was luminous, rising up out of the night fields. I turned into a field and kept running, branches scratching my face and arms, until I thumped down on the ground, palms in the dirt. I breathed. Then I jumped up and was off again. I came out of the fields to the streets. I rushed up and down until I came on our hostel at last. I walked through the atrium, still empty of Internacionalistas, back to our room, back to George. I leaned against the door. I slid down it, waited. I turned on my side and lay on the cement. Waited.

What I remember most about waiting there on the cement is the water standing all around, shining circles that reflected the light.

We lived in zones in Managua and in order to save water during the shortage, the government turned it off two days a week, and which days you had no water depended on what zone you were in. The Internacionalistas always became very animated about not having water. The night before, the *dueña* of the hostel would fill container after container with water—tubs and jugs and bottles and buckets—and set them out for the Internacionalistas. Water stood all over and still we were very pleased about having no water. Sometimes the city didn't shut the water off until seven or eight in the morning, so if you woke early you could still have a shower, but on the day the water was off in your zone you were ready not to take a shower. You were ready not to brush your teeth. You drank beer or Rojita all day because it was better to save what water you had. By afternoon the standing water was squirming with bugs, and small clouds of mosquitoes hung over the buckets. The water attracted mosquitoes. In Panama, tens of thousands of people died of yellow fever, malaria, and dengue from standing water during the French effort to build the canal. We all knew that and talked about it, shaking our heads, and yet it never occurred to us to cover our water.

The day I broke the engagement and was nearly attacked or at least mistaken for a prostitute was a day we were supposed to have no water. But the government hadn't turned it off. They'd gotten the day mixed up or they were trying to be nice or it was another sign that things were getting a little chaotic behind the curtain. We'd prepared for a day without water, but it was all around us and coming out of the faucets. Its seamless presence felt abundant, extreme even. We hadn't realized how much we'd missed it when it wasn't there.

CENSORSHIP

George and I were in Managua the day *La Prensa* reopened. We were there to read the first paper off the presses.

The Sandinistas had shut the paper down years before, saying at *La Prensa* they took money from the CIA and didn't like the revolution. Opponents called it censorship—more proof of Sandinista Communist treachery. Look at the Russians, look at the Cubans. Now the Sandinistas. But the Sandinistas were letting *La Prensa* reopen. What did it mean? The Internacionalistas took it as a sign of triumph (*¡Viva Sandino!*), but maybe it was another sign of ruin.

I remember being on the street when the paper came off the presses—the crowds of people, the newspaper boy turning in circles, his thin papers going from his fingers, passing through the crowd. It was late in our trip. I'm not sure about the timing. We were still planning to get married at that point, but we were uncomfortable and I was about to say I didn't want to. Or maybe we weren't going to get married anymore and that's why we were uncomfortable, not sure what we were to each other now. I'm certain it was our second time in Nicaragua. We were pinging around, an arsenal of interviews in our bags. I know we were together and that we were unhappy. But on that day the talk was

all about *La Prensa*. It was afternoon, the day *La Prensa* reopened.
The newspaper got a late start or their boy did. I don't recall what
was in the paper, what the articles were about, but I know I was
surprised. I had thought it was a heroic moment, a historic one. I
had thought *La Prensa* might want to be at least a little nice to the
Sandinistas for letting them print their paper again, but no, at *La
Prensa* they were mad. Somebody had taken away their land,
their money, their men, made them drive taxis. They had a lot to
say about it.

Or were we someplace else that day, the day *La Prensa* reopened?
In Panama? And what I remember is the first time George and I
bought the paper, on our way back through, though it had reopened
weeks before?

Am I inventing the crowds? No, that part must be right. I can
see the people gathering, the Nicaraguan men and women, but I
can't see the rest of the day around it.

It could have been the day I vomited on the street. Or it could
have been the day I cut the soldiers' hair. Or the day I was robbed
on the bus. Or the day we went to the Russian ballet. Or the day
we interviewed the bishop. We could have been walking out the
church doors. I believe we were leaving some formidable spot—or
does the memory of formidability come from the advent of *La
Prensa*?

And now, today, I read that *La Prensa* hadn't been shut down
for years. In this book it says that the press had opened and shut
and opened and shut like a drawer during those years of the revolution. I ask a Nicaraguan journalist I meet and she confirms it.
"Did it open and close?" I say.

"Many times," she says solemnly.

So why that day all the hoopla? Was every time it reopened
a special time? And I'm misremembering its uniqueness, not

the celebration? Which part of this am I wrong about? I couldn't say. I am sure of this much: I was there in some way. I bought *La Prensa*. "Let me see it," said George, but I kept it. I held it in my hands and read the insides. Later we used it for toilet paper.

PEANUT BUTTER

George and I got separate rooms. The engagement was off, after all, but we told each other we needed separate beds in order to get some sleep. The beds were singles and we were sick and hot. The rooms cost two dollars apiece. We split up our stuff and George went into one room on one side of the atrium and I went into another on the other and that was it for a while. I lay alone in the concrete room. Days passed. One morning I got up and went to his room. It was empty, cleaned out, and I figured we'd broken up and he'd taken off, left me there. I went back to my room and got onto the bed.

I lay there sweating for days. I didn't eat. A huge spider lived in the room—flat and fast, the size of a small plate. Now and then it came out, sat on the wall, and then scooted away. I watched for it and threw shoes its way but didn't get it and I lived in low-steam fear. The Internacionalistas talked all day and night outside my room. They sat at plastic white tables that they moved around to try to stay in the shade. They'd start out in the morning at one end of the atrium, and as the day went on and the sun moved across the sky, they moved the tables and chairs across the cement to the other end. The next morning they'd carry the tables back and start over. I watched this all day. I had to leave the door to my room open a little because the roof was a strip of corrugated tin and the room worked like a convection oven.

One day an Internacionalista put his head into my room.

"What do you do in here?" he said.

"Go away. I'm sick."

In fact I wasn't sure if I was still sick. I'd felt the way I felt—sickish—for so long that I didn't know if it was illness or if this was just what I was, if this was me being normal and normal for me was sickish.

"What is wrong with you?"

"I don't know."

He was some sort of European. The young blond kind who speaks perfect English. "Come out," he said. "I'm tired seeing you in here."

"How do you think I feel?"

"I walk by the same room, see the same person. I feel like I repeat myself."

"That's life, buddy."

He walked in and looked down at me on my bed. "Did you see a doctor? You can see the doctor here for very cheap."

"You better get out of here. My boyfriend's coming back," I said.

"What boyfriend. No one comes in here."

Maybe I should have been nervous at this point, but I was used to being approached by men of all ethnicities and ages, inside and outside these hostels. I just tugged my dress over my knees. I was wearing my "fruit basket" dress, so-called because of the pictures of large dark fruits on it. I had begun wearing it every single day. One day I washed it and all the Internacionalistas in the hostel congratulated me and told me how nice I looked and said that I should try a trick like that more often.

"Let's go to the movies," said the guy.

"There are no movies."

"Sure there are movies."

"You're thinking of Mexico. You're thinking of Spain."

"I will take you to eat an ice cream then." He reached out to touch my leg and I kicked his hand away.

"I know that place," I said. "Every day they say they have a different flavor. Some days they say chocolate. Some days they say strawberry. But it's vanilla. Vanilla every day." That place drove me crazy. In one place we stayed someone had written on the wall of our room, *"La vida es tan corta comer helados vanillos y bailer con hombres aburridos."* Life is too short to eat vanilla ice cream and dance with boring men.

"Forget this town," he said. "Let's go to India. They have beautiful rugs in India. We can lie on them and look at the sky."

After all these years, I still remember the thing that impressed him most about India was the rugs. I don't even know what he was talking about. I've never been to India and no one else I've met who has gone has mentioned the rugs as the high point of their Indian adventure, though I'm sure there are indeed beautiful rugs to be found in that country.

"No thanks," was what I told this guy. I'd say the same thing today.

"Okay," he said. "I will bring you to my parents' house."

"Why would I go there?"

"It's very nice." He drew the house in the air. "It's full of rooms."

"What do I want with rooms?" I said. "I've got a room."

He dropped his hands. "I can't go back without you."

We'd reached an impasse. I wasn't going with him, but he wouldn't leave unless I went. He bowed his head like in prayer. He closed his eyes.

"Tell you what you can do," I said. "You could go get me some peanut butter."

He opened his eyes. "You know where to get peanut butter?"

"Black market," I said. "Military packets. There's a place. I'll tell you how to get there, but you have to promise to bring me some. Promise?"

"Tell me where first."

"Promise first."

"Tell first."

"Promise first."

He sat down on the floor. He put his head between his knees. "I am sick of this revolution," he said.

SMALLER

It was in that room that I began having a dream I then had for years. I dreamed Central America was shrinking. It happened fast. I was standing on it and then suddenly it got smaller. I teetered for a moment, nearly fell, then planted my feet in Nicaragua, my heel sunk in Lake Nicaragua. I crouched and saw George among the plastic trees, the tiny metal towers. Solid black lines separated the countries. I reached in for George, but the ground beneath me shook—an earthquake?—and Central America shrank again. I couldn't stand on it anymore. I fell into the ocean and was left tossing around with my pack. I didn't see George. I grabbed hold of Costa Rica, tried to wrap a leg around it, throw my pack on top, but my pack had opened. My things were falling into the water. I was grabbing my belongings, getting them back into my pack—my guidebook, my bottle of shampoo—but everything was muddy or lost. The water was too deep to splash home on foot. I'd have to swim, but I couldn't go without George, and how would I carry my pack? It would get soaked, was already soaked. Central America shook again, another earthquake, and I was thrown into the sea, head under, now above, sky overhead. My pack had sunk and George was gone.

I had the dream on and off for many years. I'd wake and sometimes if a fan was whirling or if the light was coming in on a certain slant, I thought I was back. I'd sit up—where's George? Instead of a shabby square of bed, our stuff in collapse on the floor, I'd find the room spread cleanly around me, a lamp, a desk, a closet. At some point the dream stopped. I don't know why.

In the final scene of the dream I'd try to swim toward Central America but it was far away now, growing smaller and smaller. It squeezed to a dot and disappeared.

FORGETTABLE MOMENTS

George came back. One day I returned from the toilets and he was standing over my bed.

"Our visas are about to expire," he said. He had some mosquito coils and my flashlight in his hands. "We have to get out of here. It's time to go."

Then I saw. He had my backpack out.

"You came back," I said.

"What?" he said tiredly. "What are you talking about?"

I looked at him for a while. Hadn't we broken up and he'd left? Hadn't I been abandoned? Or was it possible, I wondered, that he'd been in the hostel all this time? Had I looked for him in the wrong room? Had he not abandoned me at all?

Had we not even broken up?

Or had we broken up, separated, ended things once and for all, but neither of us even managed to make it off the premises? It could be that's what happened.

It's impossible to know what another person's important moments are, the few moments they'll always remember in the deep ocean of all the ones they'll forget. Was that an important moment for him—showing up after leaving me or not leaving me there in that hostel?

If I could talk to George again, just once, I would say, "Okay, here's a pen. First question. Write down the ten most important moments in your life."

"Trick question," he would say. "You just want to know if you would be on the list—which how could you be? You can't imagine all the things I've done. It's been more than twenty years."

"Okay," I would say. "Fair enough. New question. Write down the ten most important moments from that trip."

There's no way that moment wouldn't be on the list, the moment he returned after leaving me or not leaving me, when he knew where I was and I didn't know where he was and still he chose not to come. It wasn't punishment on his part, leaving me like that, if he even did. That kind of behavior wasn't in him. He wasn't mean or manipulative or vengeful. He was a man who acted not by volition, but drive. If he left, he did it because he had to, and if he came back, it was because of the same. I never asked him where he was those days we were apart. No matter if he was in the next room in bed or walking down a road two days away— maybe he doesn't even remember today—still, I know how it was for him. I know what it is to not know what to do, to choose when you don't want any of the options left open to you, to be on a path when it feels like any path is a mistake.

What I didn't realize at that moment, with my belongings tossed out on the bed, is that I had turned a little strange on this trip. The next year I'd go back to school and feel a little strange around all my healthy, rosy-cheeked classmates. It was strange to be strange and I'd do what I had to to stop, not because I wanted what was on the other side of strange, but because both sides, all sides, looked like mistakes. The next year I felt a little less strange and what was around me was less strange, the year after that still less, and finally one day there I was—nothing around me was strange and I wasn't strange. I was normal.

But George stayed strange. He'd wait around for a couple of years, maybe trying not to be strange, maybe not trying. I moved out of our apartment, saying I had to "find myself," which at first made George laugh but later did not. It would turn out to be harder to find myself than I expected because so little of me existed to begin with. George tried to stick it out until I found myself, but finally he just couldn't. It was taking too long. One day he came over to my place and said he wanted to say good-bye. He was leaving, had to. He hadn't been over in a while, and in that moment he looked much like he did that day in Managua— determined, ill-at-ease in the middle of a room that was clearly mine, not ours. Only this time he wasn't coming back to fetch me. Instead he was leaving for good. He glanced around the room. "Wow," he said. "Look at all this stuff you've got. You've got a lot of stuff now." A few minutes later he was gone.

So that's how it would end. But on that day in November 1987, he came back for me, or hadn't left without me in the first place. He gathered me up, found or not, and scooped up my stuff, which was still only a pack's worth, and we left Managua together again—out of duty, perhaps, or habit, or fear, or sheer stubbornness, or because we'd have to both go back the same way in any case. Many people travel together on thinner threads than that: because they happened to get on the same bus a town or two back, or because they have complementary guidebooks, or they both speak French.

We put our things away and rode out of Managua that night. We still had a few more adventures to go, though we didn't know that yet. We headed for the border, our backpacks slung up on top of the bus, side by side, a sky full of water. Just like that, we were going home.

WHAT HAPPENED TO GEORGE

As a matter of fact I didn't have much stuff the day George came to say good-bye. I still feel a little particular on this point. Sure, I had the normal apartment appliances that come with an apartment, oven and cabinets and doors, but I didn't own those. I had some boxes of kitchenware, a few stools and chairs strewn around, clothes.

No proper revolutionary would cart around a lot of stuff even if she had quit and gone home.

As for George, he noted my excess of belongings, then he left the States, went back through Central America, where all the revolutions were ending one by one, falling over like buildings, and where the U.S. Army was lifting Noriega out of Panama with a crane. George continued on through the Darien Gap, where the road narrows like a funnel and disappears into rain forest and mud, and the earth becomes water as you walk. He came out on the other side in the vast land of South America. He traveled around, much as he and I had together. I stayed behind.

In Brazil he fell in love. He didn't use the words "fell in love" when he told me about it years later on the phone. He said he met "the queen of the peasants." To this day I have no idea what that means—crown, rags, a path winding through a shantytown, who knows what he was talking about.

He proposed—to her, of course.

Apparently the queen of the peasants had to have her father's permission because her father wouldn't give it. "Not unless you have a house to put her in," he said. George didn't have any money, of course. Never had a dime in his life. So he returned to the States and worked all day pouring cement and lifting buckets and setting them down, and at night he delivered pizzas to the homes of our civilians. He went back to Brazil and bought a large piece of land.

"There," he said to the father, "now may I marry your daughter?"

The father said, "I don't see a house to put her in."

So again George returned to the States and again saved up money and went back to Brazil and built a house on his land. Then he said to the father, "Look, you see? A house. Now may I marry your daughter?" And the father couldn't speak, so awed was he by their love. George married that peasant queen and put her in the house, and when she had his baby, he put the baby in the house too.

He told me all this on the phone. We were on the phone because I tracked him down and called him once when I heard he was back in the States. I don't know what year this was—maybe '96 or '97? I still hadn't found myself.

"What do you do in Brazil?" I asked him.

"Nothing," he said.

"But you must do something."

"We owned a bar for a while," he said, "but we traded it for a TV set."

So there it is: He married a queen. They have a baby and a TV set. They watch their game shows and look out the window at the rain.

"But what else are you going to do?" I said.

"Nothing," he said. "I'm not going to do anything."

"Nothing?"

"Maybe I'll write a book," he said.

For years I looked for that book. I waited and waited.

That's all I knew of him for a long time—the queen and the baby and the book I was waiting for, that he would write by the blue light of the TV.

PART FIVE

COMMON HUMAN FATES

STUFF

"So George went off and had a blissful life in the jungle and you wound up with a lot of stuff. Is that what you're saying?"

"No, I *didn't* have a lot of stuff. He said I did, but I didn't."

"Well, get some stuff then, if that's what you want," the guy says. He nods to the bartender for another.

"No, I mean, I have plenty of stuff now."

"So what's the problem? You have your own house now, a house full of stuff."

"Actually, no, I don't have a house. I live in someone else's house. Part of someone else's house, an apartment, really."

"All right, name the things you have."

"Car. Clothes. Lamp. Plant."

"That sounds like plenty of stuff." He sips at the foam, eyes the shrilly game overhead.

"It is. I said that already."

"Name the things you don't have."

"I don't know why I'm talking to you," I say. "There's a whole world out there I don't have."

"Name them."

SANDINO IN THE SKY

The first time I went back to Nicaragua was the summer of 2000, wet-season Managua, mornings of hot haze, then insane rain, then the heavy evenings of heat and damp leaves. I wasn't sure why I was back. I'd come up with the idea of interviewing people, the way George and I had. It was a good idea. People I told the idea to said it was interesting and they seemed impressed. I'd look for those revolutionaries, the old priests and their followers—whatever happened to those guys?

I put on my sun hat one morning and walked over to the Hotel Intercontinental. There's a hill behind it and I began a plodding ascent in the heat, slowly rising over flat-faced Managua. The president had put up billboards with his name on them, everywhere you looked, all over the city, and if you rode out to the countryside, you'd see them there too, beside the humblest shacks, along the oldest roads, emerging from the dust clouds: Arnoldo Alemán.

"This is boring," said my sister.

Did I mention I'd brought my sister with me? Yes, that was another part of the plan. I was going to teach my little sister about the revolution. She hadn't known that was the plan—she'd had in mind beach songs and sand—and because I am her big sister I didn't know she didn't know. She and I were just beginning to understand this misunderstanding.

We kept climbing the hill. It took a long time and it was hot. At last we came to the gigantic statue of Sandino. It shot straight up into the sky. During the revolution the Sandinistas had put up their own statues in the plaza, ones to represent the times: men with machine guns, of course. And they'd put a giant silhouette of Sandino himself in his big hat on top of the hill behind el Inter. It's still there.

"Would you look at that," I said to my sister. "General Sandino. Inspired the revolution."

I told her a little anecdote about him, how in a battle against a white man he'd refused to surrender, and somebody had to explain it to the president. I didn't tell it right. My sister had the look that said she didn't care who that guy was.

A soldier with a machine gun was standing under the statue. "See that?" I said. "There's a real live soldier too." We went over to him.

"What are you doing?" I said.

"Guarding Sandino," said the soldier.

"From what?"

"Graffiti."

"Oh."

My sister looked disappointed.

"Soldiers guard many strange things," I told her. "Bushes, abandoned houses, empty beaches, blocks of wood, walls of sacks . . ."

We turned to go.

"But it's lonely," the soldier called to us. "I stand here by myself all day. Do you see the lizards around? As big as cats."

"Yes, we saw them," said my sister, who also speaks Spanish. "They walk like dogs."

"They don't walk like dogs," I corrected her. "If anything, they walk like crocodiles. Or maybe insects, not dogs."

Below us el Inter sat. In a few more years, it wouldn't be "el Inter" anymore. It'd be sold off, abandoned, reclaimed, renamed: the Crowne Plaza, fixed up, revamped, but by then the second hotel in town. There'd be a new Intercontinental, a nicer Intercontinental, brighter, more elegant, closer to the plaza. Any more revolutions go on, the journalists are going to want to stay at that one instead. Things keep going this way and one day we won't have el Inter anymore. Its doors will close for good and that, for me, will be the very end of the revolution. But back in 2000 it wasn't a Crowne Plaza yet. The revolution ten years done, Nicaragua on its second capitalist president, but it was still el Inter and it was open—a little grayer perhaps, a little squatter, still itself but becoming something different every minute, as every minute more history flew by and the world became something different around it, like the river Heraclitus can't step into twice. The river, all that water passing through, all that earth sliding down the bank into the silt, all the fish and plants and mold growing and dying inside, all the cities going up around it or falling down into it.

There's a fuzziness to what I know about George. The marks I can make are incomplete. I don't have the dates, for example, of when he went back to claim the peasant queen, when he built the house. I lost some years somewhere. At one point, before the TV set, someone had told me he was at seminary or divinity school. He'd won a fellowship to Harvard or Yale. Then I heard he'd dropped out, that he'd had a sudden awakening and left, or maybe it was that he'd grown slowly disillusioned and had been kicked out.

This must have been the year he was between jobs at the pizza joint, between shifts on the construction line.

Perhaps that year he'd been trying to forget the peasant queen. Perhaps he'd been trying to live—how do you say it?—"up to his potential"? I've always had misgivings about that phrase. Why should studying at Harvard be more thoroughly "living up to his potential" than watching TV in the rain forests of Brazil? I imagine he would agree with me on this point (he's the one who taught me it in the first place) since he left Harvard or Yale or was told to leave and then went back to claim his queen.

The year 2000 may have been the lowest year of my life. I didn't know what I was doing. I was trying to be a writer by that time, but it wasn't working out. I'd come home to my crappy Chicago apartment, feeling sorry for myself, and have to pry open a mailbox stuffed with rejection letters. I was midway through a demented, dismal romance that I couldn't bring myself to end. My boyfriend hated me and avoided me at all costs. I loved him desperately and wanted only to be near him. I was teaching five or six classes a semester at four different schools. I drove all over the city, my grammar books tossed in the backseat. I was teaching on Saturdays in the suburbs, Monday mornings downtown, writing in the middle of the night for a magazine that pitched new age health products, and hopefully a few lines of my own. I couldn't make enough to pay rent in a slum. I'd come home and find my electric off one day, my phone off another. I'd have to figure out if I hadn't paid my bill or if the wiring in the building had gone off (again), or was the whole block down tonight? One cold month I had no hot water. My neighbors fought day and night on what seemed like rotation. I'd go out to the street and find all the windows of my car smashed or the tires slashed or my license plates gone. Once a man grabbed me from behind outside my apartment and I screamed him away. My family, all of them without exception, thought I was a bum and told me so every time they saw me. "It's sad what's happened to you," they said. "Just sad."

I'd had it. I mean, I had really had it. But what was I going to do? You can't just give up. Or sure, you can give up, over and over, you can lie there stopped, but you start back up again, you stubborn winding clock, because the heart keeps beating, madly, wretchedly, gratefully, unless you figure out how to stop it. I could see no way out of this mess. I'd obviously missed out on an essential lesson everyone else had had. I was lacking some basic instinct, some secret understanding, the right way to believe in the American dream. I tried to think of a time when I felt at home in the world, and I came up with nothing. Then I remembered Nicaragua.

There's the foot too, of course. If you're looking at the river, knowing it's different, and looking at the world around the river and knowing that's different, you may happen to notice the foot that's stepping in the river as well. Maybe you didn't even know it was the foot you came to see, not the river, until you see the foot there, wet in the water. Then you say: Damn, what happened to that foot?

So that's where we all were that year, the tenth anniversary of the revolution's end: the Sandinistas driving taxis around the city, their leaders becoming corrupt, me coming apart and shaking out a trail of debris, George in the jungle watching TV.

"There's so many of you," said the soldier in charge of Sandino. "What do you come here for?"

My sister and I looked at each other.

"Well, I've been here before, you see," I said.

"Why do you want to go back to the same place?" he said.

I didn't know how to answer that.

"I think I'd want to see someplace else," he said.

WHERE THE DANES STAYED

"Old Nica, Nica of the revolution, those were the days. It's sure not like it used to be. The fun we had."

"Remember the water?"

"Oh, the water, the districts, the two days a week."

"It smelled like chlorine."

"What fun that was."

"And Comedor Sarah!"

"You know, she's not around anymore, trying to sell the place."

We shook our heads.

It was a year later, 2001. I was back in Nicaragua. Again. I had no reason to be there and I didn't have the money for it, but I was back. I'd gone looking for Comedor Sarah that day, walking *una cuadra arriba, dos cuadras al lago* all over the place, until a kid on the street told me, "*Ya no está.*" Of course it wasn't. It seemed absurd that *I* was there, that I was still me, that I hadn't died by now and been reincarnated and returned to Nicaragua as a turtle. That's how long ago it all seemed. But no, I was still me. I'd found another former Internacionalista, in fact, a European. We can't keep away.

He and I were settled in the hotel atrium with a bottle of rum.

"Remember the Russians? The AK-40s?"

"Ah, the Russians, they loved American stuff. Movies and food."

"The córdobas!"

"You had to carry bags of them everywhere you went."

We raised our hands to show the bags of córdobas we had to carry.

"Remember Molinitos?"

"Molinitos, what is that?"

"Molinitos."

We frowned at each other over the rum.

"You know, Molinitos. A pension. It was right around the corner."

"I don't remember that."

"You remember. All the Danes stayed there."

"Danes?"

"Sure."

"I don't remember any Danes anywhere."

"Sure."

"No."

There were some Peace Corps volunteers being silly in the corner, smashing bottles into the trash can, throwing them from a distance.

"Well, they were here."

He and I were sitting in the Hotel Oye, five bucks a night. There were two sets of water pipes, one line beside the other in every bathroom, over every sink. One of the lines didn't work, but nobody bothered to pull the dead one out, so two pipes ran up the wall and there were two showerheads in every shower. You had to try both faucets. The entire hotel was built with this philosophy. The rafters were a mess of metal and wood. Wooden beams swung loosely. Unfinished paintings sat on the floor. Projects started and were deserted. People stripped off the pieces they needed and left the rest swinging half-attached, like a rejected thought, no longer in use but still there. The electric wiring hung in a jumble from the ceiling, strung across the wall. It was held together with bits of black electrical tape, here wrapped around a curtain rod, there forming a spiderweb on the ceiling, suspended like a trapeze net.

What can we say? We tried to join the wrong revolution. For ten different reasons we were wrong: it wasn't ours, it didn't work, we didn't understand it.

He and I had finished the rum and were lying on our chairs like lizards. All these years and I felt like I hadn't moved on at all.

"Remember Nicaragua of the revolution? Everyone was so excited."

"I tell the people at home. I tell them Nicaragua is still beautiful! You shouldn't abandon old friends."

"Old friends shouldn't abandon you either."

I wasn't sure what he was talking about there, but after that rum I was ready to back him up a hundred percent. Damn it, old friends *shouldn't* abandon you.

THREE BOATS

One of my final adventures with George was on a boat. He said we'd take a vacation—a boat, like a cruise. This was right after the broken engagement, right after he left or didn't leave and I lay on the bed looking at the walls, right after we managed to make it out of Managua. We still needed to figure out a different way back to the States. We didn't have enough money to return the way we'd come. We sat in a room in a hot border town, George calculating shortcuts and not explaining them to me, and me being mad about it and about anything else I could think of. I pointed out that we could go this way (I drew a line on the map with my thumb) and get back to the States through Texas and then hitchhike the rest of the way.

"We're not going to Texas," George said.

George wouldn't go to Texas. He'd once sworn he never would. He had a couple of cousins from Texas whom he teased every time they came to town. Texas was so dumb, George had told his cousins, that anyone who went to Texas would be suddenly struck with stupidity, which explained why the cousins were so dumb. He'd made a pledge never to go to Texas. It was all part of a childhood joke from long ago. He still thought it was funny and wouldn't go.

He'd always been like that. Anyone who knows him who hears this story will say, "That's George for you," and shrug. But in fact, that one time he and I spoke on the phone, he told me he'd been to Texas. "Can you believe it?" he said. "I had no choice. I had to cut through Texas."

"Really," I said.

I'd thought at the time that we had no choice.

I bet those cousins weren't even that dumb.

George said the shortest way back was by water. We could cross to some islands off the coast of Honduras and get back to the mainland by way of Belize and cut off one large leg of the trip. Then he said the bit about it being a vacation, an island holiday— boat ride, Caribbean sun, umbrellas in the sand. So we went to the coast and found a cheap boat, a discount boat, so small that George and I were the only passengers, and it sank low in the water when he and I got on.

At first the ride wasn't bad. The water was calm and dolphins jumped alongside the boat as it pulled into the sea. The fisherman held out his hand for them to leap at. But then the sky clouded over and the wind came up and waves began to hit the little boat. We tilted, smacked the waves, and jumped, slammed back into the water over and over. I huddled down on the floor of the boat and held on to my seat with both hands to keep from flying off. I bit my lip so as not to throw up. Water spilled over the side in bucketfuls. George bailed with a tin bowl like a machine and the fisherman was shouting. Then the rain came, drowning the boat. I couldn't tell the difference between the sea and the air. I was soaked, had seaweed in my fingers, my hair. The fisherman began shoving barrels over the side. George was trying to bail but fell over. I rose to help, but the fisherman pushed me down with a hard shove. This is it, I thought. I'm going to die and it's all George's fault.

But then the rain died down. Far off, lights blinked like fireflies in the fog. Somehow the shore appeared, a gray mass between the sea and sky. I felt the fisherman lifting me under the arms and setting me on the wet dock.

"That's not the worst," a man said.

"What?" I said.

His face emerged from behind a T-shirt—the room doubled as a laundry and dine-in. Clothes hung on lines down the room. I was in a hostel in Costa Rica in 2002, still hanging around Central America. The man said again, "That's not the worst." He looked Indian and spoke like the queen, and I didn't think he was very friendly. I hadn't said my story was the worst and I wouldn't have told it at all except someone asked if I'd been to the islands off Honduras and I didn't know how to answer except to describe one location after another, draw the line that led to the point.

Once I started going back to Nicaragua, I couldn't stop. I was like a train heading off the side of a mountain into the sea. I broke off relationships, quit jobs. I could live for ten dollars a day. I went back to El Salvador, back to Panama. I stayed away longer and longer. It was turning into years of this nonsense now. I couldn't figure out what I was doing there and it became more and more uncomfortable as I tried to explain.

"Not the worst?" said another tourist. "I suppose it could have been worse if she drowned."

So at least someone was on my side.

"If you want to hear the worst, I could tell you," said the man.

"And how are you supposed to know the worst?" I said.

"I went through it myself," he said.

The tourists at the table turned to listen.

"I boated those same waters," said the man, "only one month ago today. I was one of twelve scientists. We hired a boat to take us to Honduras. Just like you, the sky was beautiful and clear."

The tourists nodded to each other. "Scientists, well!"

(What are scientists always doing on boats? And what's the use of twelve of them? The boat I'd been on could not have held twelve people and, as all sailors know, the smaller the boat, the worse the trip.)

"Halfway there, the first engine gave out," he said. "The captain came out to let us know. We weren't too worried because there was a second engine."

(Two engines? Our boat had an engine the size of a stapler.)

"Just like you, the water turned choppy. The captain came out and said to put on the life jackets. We didn't know if this was good news because that meant there were life jackets or bad news because we might need them. Then the sea became violent. Water was coming over the sides in tubfuls. We were soaked, all our suitcases like they'd fallen into the ocean. Still, the storm grew worse. We were seasick, throwing up over the side. The captain yelled for us all to run to one side of the boat. Then he'd yell, '¡El otro lado!' and we'd all run back and so on, to keep us from capsizing."

(Doesn't sound so bad, running up and down like a relay.)

"Then it looked like we might make it. Far away, four kilometers or so, we could see land. Then the second engine gave out."

The tourists at the table sucked in their breath.

(Who was this guy, Candide?)

The man nodded. "So close to land. The captain took a life jacket and waved it in the air on a stick. 'What the hell are you doing?' we said to him. 'You think someone's going to see that?' Some of the scientists had whistles and blew them, six short blasts, the international help signal."

(Only a dozen scientists would know the international help signal on a whistle.)

"No one came. It began to get dark. We took out our torches and flashed our lights at the shore. Still, no one came. Some of us started saying we should swim. The captain said, 'No, no, you can't possibly. This sea is full of sharks.' We waited, each moment drifting farther from land. Finally two of our men said, 'Well, bugger this,' and dove into the water. They towed the boat with ropes, swam four kilometers to shore, in shark-infested water."

The tourists let their breath out. "Oh, that's certainly the worst," they said.

The man held up a hand. "Our luck, the compass was broken. We arrived at an abandoned beach far from the docks. We pulled the boat up until it stuck in the sand and then we waded to shore. We hiked through jungle and swamp for two hours in the dark and the rain to reach town. Then we pounded on the immigration officer's door at midnight and woke him up. 'You have to stamp these passports,' we said. 'We've just entered the country.'"

The tourists shook their heads. "Did you get a discount on the boat ride?" one said. "After all, you had to swim to shore."

"Not even a discount," said the man.

The tourists at the table looked over at me. Not even a discount.

But hey, I never said mine was the worst.

Two bad boat tales must be balanced by one good boat tale, so say sailors. (Do sailors say that? I don't know. I've never known a sailor.) The third boat tale begins in 2003, ten months after the Indian man told the story of the worst. It was the latest of night, and I was with a friend paddling in quiet water off the coast of Costa Rica, way at the end of it, almost in Panama. Our canoe was barely big enough for the two of us. We drifted down a thin inlet through the rain forest. We became fastened to the foliage now and then, stuck in the mud, and our paddles helped push us over the shrub. There'd been a hurricane a few days before and giant leaves blocked the path in places, like bridges, and we had to knock them aside to get by. For once it wasn't raining and the night sky shine came through the trees. We reached the end of the inlet and floated out into the sea.

It was the last night of my sojourns south. I was going home. I'm not sure how I knew that. The feeling had been coming on for months already, a year, years. Maybe I'd known since 1987 that a piece of me had stayed behind, snagged in Central America, fastened to the foliage, and someday I'd have to get it and bring it back or else unhook it and leave it there alone. All I can say for sure is that each day held a new small awakening or disillusionment (sometimes those two are closer than you'd think, sometimes the awakening *is* the disillusion—*Oh, I see, this isn't going to work at all.*).

One day I woke on a beach with sand in my hair and thought: I'll never be who I was then.

One day I found myself sitting alone at a table of strangers and I thought: I can't go back into the past and start over. I have to just muddle on from where I am.

Another day I was sitting in a church, birds screaming in their nests in the columns, and I thought: What am I doing here? I can't hide here forever, for Christ's sake.

I'm bored out of my skull, I thought.

Each day was like that, small understanding built on small understanding, until one day I thought: It's time to go home. Build a life in the United States. The longer I stay away, the less there is to go home to. Only fear keeps me gone.

I saw it as clearly and cleverly as if I'd jumped from an airplane and thought: I should pull this string.

I don't know how it was for George (who can tell another man's awakening or disillusionment?), but this is what I wonder: On his way back to Brazil, after leaving Harvard or Yale, did he feel like a failure? Did he feel lost? Did he feel afraid? However grandly it turned out in the end (TV, baby, house in the rain), did his trip back to Brazil feel at that moment not like a determined stomp, but a muddled escape?

Or did he feel certain—now was the time, he knew at last what he wanted?

The night of the third boat, the sea was the calmest I've ever seen it. Like it was holding its breath or sleeping. Or hanging back, pausing in its turmoil (that echoes our own fuss) to watch and wave two boaters to shore. The moon was strong and our paddles looked like they were scooping cups of pale light out of the dark water. We boated over the sea with our moon paddles toward the shore.

There would still be years of difficulty to get through. And I didn't even know how much I was going to miss this wet air, this living water, the roosters sounding hoarse and imperfect, the parrots with their warped alien imitations, the falling banana leaves, these voices. I didn't even know how hard it was going to be for me to do what seemed like just a few simple things—get a job, write a book, write another book, find a kind boyfriend, find a way back to my family—but I'd do them.

I got out of the boat and said good-bye to my friend. I walked through the pebbled water to the shore, stood at the bus stop, and waited for dawn. Then I took a series of buses to San Jose and flew back to the United States.

GOOD SPORT

The very last bus of the trip. George and I got on and headed for Nogales.

We were riding along through the desert plants, which were green but a muted green, so muted they felt like brown, like a barely hanging-on green. Beyond the not-green green were the mountains, a purple stain on the sky. If you could look into the bus, could zoom in on our positions across all this time and space, if you could see our faces and the way we held our bodies, you would see that one of us was eager and ready to go home, one of us was not. One of us was already alienated but trying to be a good sport about it and would try to be that way for several years more—a good sport—but finally give up. I thought I knew which of us was which for a long time, but it's unclear to me today.

Did George ever feel at home anywhere again? No, I bet he couldn't. Wherever he went, wherever he is, part of him feels apart. He had changed and couldn't fit in at home anymore, even in the uncomfortable wrong-puzzle-piece way that he had in the first place. But he didn't feel at home anywhere else either. It did eventually get better for him, but the feeling of loneliness never went away, though he finally got used to it.

You can be a lot of things and be lonely. You can do exciting things and be lonely. You can fall in love and be lonely. You can marry and have children and be lonely. You can be content and be lonely. Once you've felt that kind of deep alienation, it changes you permanently. Permanent change means a lack of full recovery. If a man has an accident and limps for the rest of his life, we say he never fully recovered. You can even be lonely and be lonely.

It's not that I knew George so well that even after not speaking to him for all these years I think I still know who he is and how he feels. It's just that I've known so many others like him. I could tell dozens of stories like his. These are just common human fates. We hobble along in that damaged state and live all kinds of lives afterward.

The last bus of the trip pulled into the Nogales station. George had slept through the desert, and I had the McDonald's to look forward to, on the other side of the border. My father and mother and sister were waiting at the station. I could see them out the window. They were waving to me with the awkwardness of strangers.

Back in the States, the hot water felt odd, unfresh at first. I wasn't used to it and didn't like it. That first week, I saw a line of women walking toward me and I thought it was a protest—but no, those white squares they had were bags, not signs, I realized. It wasn't a revolution. It was shopping.

I stayed with my family for a few weeks and I felt like a visitor in their house. They had moved to Arizona and I had never lived in that state. We all regarded one another with caution. I overheard my sister whispering questions about me to my mother—why did I keep the toothpaste in the shower? I was indignant. I'd always kept my toothpaste in the shower! My father would barely speak to me, except to shout. And I was impossible, had out all my religious craziness on the table and I heaped it on them. I pulled away, constructed a giant barricade they'd have to somehow get over or around if they wanted to see me at all. They sent me back to school and I went down into the college undertow, felt a little less strange each year.

IN THE MOVIE OF YOUR LIFE

In fact, there was a fourth boat.

Once we got back, I stayed in the United States. Didn't want to go anywhere, not Europe, not Canada, certainly not anywhere south. George wandered off without me.

When I finally did leave, it was only because my parents talked me into it. They were going on a cruise with some friends and they invited me along. Mexico Sunrise Cruiseline or some such. It was cheap, a group package, practically free. My father had embarked that year on his long campaign to get close to me, although I hadn't noticed yet—no easy operation on his part, but it did eventually work. How they got me to go on a cruise is a mystery. The worst vacation of my life. My parents' friends played bingo every night. The lines at the buffet were just creepy. I'd been a Communist, a revolutionary, a Christian for the liberation, and here I was, another thread in the American capitalist carpet— how humiliating. I stood muttering at the ship's rail for days. My father thought it was so funny. He kept coming up behind me and saying, "In the movie of your life, here you are, pulling into port on this cruise ship, and the caption reads: 'Five years later.'" I had to admit it was a good joke. He got a smile out of me.

FATHERS

A few months after George and I came back from fomenting the revolution, George's father left his mother. The youngest son finished high school and the father chose that moment to go. That's the kind of man he was, one who did not shirk responsibility, who stood by until the last son sallied forth, who waited until everyone was safe off the premises before he'd make his own move toward the door, to ensure that in the moment of his exit, his wife, after having cared for so many for so long, would be suddenly, absolutely alone. I didn't find out for several months, and even then I found out by accident or, more accurately, I found out by snooping while pretending to water a dying plant. George didn't tell me his father was gone. By that time, he and I were somewhat estranged. In our basement apartment George placed piles of books around his desk, so many it looked like he was building a wall. He stayed inside that walled-in space and worked on his thesis on liberation theology. I began going out at night, making new friends, going to dance clubs. George took on a job as a janitor and was gone five nights a week. Then he signed up for a night class in Denver and was gone six. Not much after that, I moved out.

I still wonder why George's father disliked George's mother so much. I never learned anything about that father. No one in the family ever told me a single story about him, except once when George's mother said to me, "He doesn't love me. He told me so." But how could that be? He must have loved her—he married her, after all. And he must have kept loving her to have had baby after baby with her, well beyond the point of extremity.

He may have stopped loving her bit by bit, as each boy was born, son after son. He seemed to be equally disgusted with all of them. Maybe he thought his sons had turned out to be a bunch of religious pansies—studying philosophy and running around on mountaintops. When they were old enough, they had weird weddings and got fake jobs and talked too much about God. Probably his wife's fault. He went to work every day without fail. The subject of God was distasteful to him. Life was disappointing.

Years later, I heard that the father was dying of brain cancer. A year after that, I heard he was dead. The brothers were finally officially fatherless for good. It must have been hard on the brothers. Maybe they were angry. A couple of them must have regretted not knowing how to know him. At least one of them (George?) must have had some stories to tell, memories of real or imagined connection with the man. I wouldn't know.

My own father did not die. I ignored him with fortitude for years. I first began to notice the change in him the same year I decided I wanted to be a writer. I was twenty-five and living with a boyfriend in Birmingham. One day my father called (this was a man who never called) and said, "I hear you want to be a writer."

"Who said that?" I said. I was ready to admit nothing.

"Every writer needs a fax machine. Let me send you one."

(This man never sent me anything.) "I don't want a fax machine," I said.

"Give me your address. I'm sending you a fax machine."

He sent me a fax machine and then he called again. "Turn on your fax machine," he said. "I'm sending you a fax."

"I don't think it works," I said. I hadn't gotten it out of the box.

"Turn it on. Here comes your fax."

So I got the fax machine out of the box. He faxed me a letter he'd written to a prisoner. He'd joined a prison reform group and had made good friends inside prison walls. The letter to my surprise was about me, about how we weren't close and that he felt it was his fault. He was sorry and full of regret. He wished we could be friends. I ignored him, and I kept on that way for another ten years, but he kept on right back, pushing away at me, again and again, until I was finally soft enough to sit next to, proving about both of us that, if nothing else, inner revolution is possible.

The one time I spoke to George—when I tracked him down and called him and he told me about the TV set and the queen—he was back in the States to attend his father's funeral. The peasant queen and his little son were there in the next room, he said.

I was saying silly things, how neat his life was, off in the jungle with a TV.

Finally he interrupted me and said irritably, "It's not perfect."

"Of course it's perfect," I said. "How is it not perfect?"

"It's just not," he said.

I thought I'd mention that.

PROPOSALS

George may have proposed to the queen of the peasants, but let's get this straight: he proposed to me first. It was my one and only marriage proposal, unless you count the four others, which I don't.

George wasn't the first man to propose to me. The first man to propose was declared insane a few days later and committed to a hospital in Chicago. I went to visit him in the special room for visitors. We sat at a white table with our hands in the table rubble— coloring books, paper coffee cups—and he became so distressed that afterward his family asked me not to come back. In any case it was more like a threat than a proposal. He looked at me in a menacing manner and said that I must marry him. After all, he said, he was the father of my child.

"That doesn't mean much," I said, "if there's no child to show for it."

"It's dead," he said.

"It wasn't a baby yet," I said. "It's not a baby if it isn't before it is."

"You killed it."

"You can't kill it if it never was."

In fact it wasn't his. The one whose it was was in jail—thirty days' time from which he emerged calling it "boring."

The second man came along a few years after George and I broke up. He and I shared an apartment in a small town full of snow. On the day he proposed, the door to the apartment had a hole in it because I had kicked it in. And the door was new because I had kicked in the first door a week before and the landlord had replaced it. And the TV was new because the man had hurled the old one across the room. But the moment of the proposal was a calm one. He and I were standing at the window, looking out at the parking lot below. He had been married three times already. He had children all over the country—children by women he had been married to and children by women he hadn't.

"Isn't this something you've tried before?" I said.

"It always works," he said. "It's fun too."

I proposed to the third man. I wasn't involved with him anymore. I had left him after he had left me after I had threatened to leave him. We were sitting alone at my aunt's kitchen table. My aunt was out of town. I said, "Let's get married," because in that moment I saw that somehow everything had gone outlandishly wrong and had stayed that way for a long time, years, and was getting worse, and if I could just marry this nice man here—suitable, quiet, kind—I might be able to set things straight.

"Half the time I don't know what you're talking about," he said.

"Half the time all the time?" I said. "Or half the time right now?"

He thought about it. "Half the time."

He left his drink on the table and went outside.

The fourth one I married. Civil war. Nine months later I was back living my normal life, alone.

THE LAST WE SAW OF GEORGE

Once, in Panama, during some of our worst times together, George and I wound up with a very tall man from French Guiana. We met him on a bus. The man had no legal visas and he was going to try to make it through all those countries and then on to Texas. There was a heartbreaking story that came along with him and a photo of a pretty wife he would one day send for. I was the bad guy here. George said he wanted to help him. George said, "It's Christian charity," and I said, "It's illegal." George said, "Obey not the laws of this earth," and I said, "I am going to vomit if I hear one more word about Jesus and all his sexist pig apostles."

The man from French Guiana sat between us and talked on and on, told us about villages he had seen, roads he had walked, his country of sun and mud.

He and George looked over his passport and papers. He had a Costa Rican visa stamp in blue ink in his passport, but it didn't look right—who knows where he'd gotten it. They did their best to fix it up.

At the border the soldiers were suspicious. These days I'm sure that they have computers to keep track of such things, but they had no computers back then. All they had were a couple of wooden shacks. The Panama side stamped us out, no problem, glad to be rid of us. The Costa Rican side kept us there for hours, pulling apart our bags, asking questions. They brought us into the shack one by one and patted us down, gave us cursory strip searches, that is, I kept my underwear on. The soldiers looked at me in my cotton underwear and thought I was pregnant. I was very thin, but I had that smooth, round stomach.

"¿Estás preñada?" a soldier said.

"No," I said. "I don't know what it is. It could be parasites."

"Or worms."

"Or malnutrition."

"Or you're pregnant."

They let us through at last. George was triumphant. He thought we could do this professionally. He tried his hand at doctoring documents for practice. Entering Nicaragua we were caught and he bribed the officer to let us go.

Later I believe he did do it professionally. He kept a car at my parents' house in Phoenix. By this time we'd broken up, I'd moved out, he'd left. His car stayed at my parents'. That first year or two he called me now and then. Once on the phone he asked if I would send him my passport. "Since you're not using it," he said. He came to get his car sometimes, then he'd bring it back. My parents let him do this. He'd be gone for a month, then he'd show up out of nowhere, get the car, bring it back late that night or the next day. One day he didn't bring it back and that was the last any of us saw of him.

PART SIX

BIG COUNTRY

PRIVATE EYE

To find him again was hard. Web searches turned up nothing. I located a brother in California and wrote to him, but he didn't write back. I guess he wasn't so eager to put me in touch with George anymore. I was clearly the ex-girlfriend now. I wrote again. I asked for George's e-mail address, tried to sound a little more professional this time, mentioned I was doing some writing about our trip. That wouldn't scare George off, right? His ex-girlfriend writes and says she's still thinking about the relationship more than twenty years later? No, no, a woman like that couldn't be trouble.

No answer. I found another brother on Facebook and tried to "friend" him, but he wouldn't be my friend. I couldn't find the other brothers.

I figured George was just flat gone now.

I thought about hiring a private eye. In fact, I spoke to a private eye. I typed into a Web search "private eye" and called the first number listed, which seemed like a bad idea as I was doing it, but the man I spoke to did not lack sense. He had reasonable ideas and asked me reasonable questions, such as, "Where do you think he is?"

"I believe," I said, "that he's in Brazil."

"Could be expensive," he said. "Big country. It could be done.

You could hire people to look for him in Brazil, but that's going to be real money."

"I have money," I said. I wasn't sure what real money was. What I had was real.

"What do you want to find him for?" the private eye said. "You know, this is not like the movies. You don't hire a private eye to find out if your wife is cheating on you. That's not what this business is."

I knew that already. It was written on his Web site. One reason that was not a good reason to hire a private eye, according to his Web site, was to find out if your wife was cheating on you.

"Do you know where he was last living?"

"I know where one of his brothers lives," I said.

"Why don't you ask his brother?"

"I wrote him and he didn't answer," I said.

"Why wouldn't he answer?"

"I know where his best friend is," I said. "His old best friend, from high school. You could call him and ask."

"Why don't you call him yourself and ask? Why wouldn't he want to hear from you?"

I called this private eye several times from different phones and pretended to be different people. I asked many questions. I didn't hire him because I was afraid how much it would cost to send him to Brazil, but I kept calling. During our last conversation he called me "Deb." I was certain I hadn't given him my name. "All right, Deb," he said. "Talk to you soon." Surely he knew it was the same woman calling over and over. I mean, the guy was a private eye. I guess he had to let me know I wasn't fooling anyone.

After that, of course, I couldn't call him again.

At last I cooked up my nerves and I called George's best friend from high school. I've always known where this guy was because he's still working at the same place he worked when he finished college, has been working there all these years. He lives right nearby the house he grew up in and does volunteer after-school tutoring at the very high school he and George had attended. I'd been following all this on the Internet for years. How do people wind up like that? I'll never know.

"You may not remember me," I said.

"I remember you," he said.

I made up an enormous mountain of crap. "My sister," I said. "She's moving. Your town. Her husband. His job. Needs advice. Schools and so on. Such and such."

"How's Wendy?" I said. "Oh that's good, that's nice. How's Max?"

"Good," I said. "Good."

"Hey," I said, "by the way, I just thought of this. Are you in touch with George? How's he doing? Still in Brazil?"

"Brazil?" the best friend said. "No, no. That was years ago. He's in Pennsylvania, isn't he? With his wife and kids."

"Pennsylvania?"

"Yeah, he's a programmer."

A *programmer*?

"Are you sure?" I said.

"Sure, I'm sure."

Now how did George learn how to be a programmer? Are there even computers in the jungles of Brazil? What does a programmer do anyway?

I'll tell you one thing. Basically I bet he has more stuff. I'd put my stuff up against his stuff any day. We could lay it out on the road, end to end, beside each other, his stuff on one side and mine on the other. We could put his kid on the road, glue him down there, any other kids he's got now too, stick them down, give his wife a chair to sit in, and his mother, who I understand is living there with them too and must be best friends with the wife. We could take apart his house, board by board, and line it on the road. There is no way he doesn't have more stuff.

A programmer!

And after his belongings and the immediate family, there are the in-laws and all that family, and don't forget the boat or canoe or trampoline in the garage, and then the garage itself. His stuff will stretch off into the distance toward the horizon and I'll be way back here on the same street I started. That's a fact.

ANOTHER ENDING

To find him again was harder. Some months went by, then some more. It wasn't fair—here I'd written this entire goddamn book. Didn't I deserve to find out a little more? I hired a private eye. Not the same private eye. That would have been humiliating. I hired a second private eye. In fact, a third private eye—the second one I spoke to charged too much and the one after that, I didn't like, and then there was another one, a fourth, who didn't call me back, so this was the *fifth* private eye. I had to sign a paper saying I wouldn't cause George any harm and that I wouldn't cause any minors or celebrities or other public figures any harm either, and that I wouldn't hire George or any minors or public figures or give them promotions, or decide not to, based on the information my private eye gave me. And I had to write a short essay about what I planned to do to George when I found him. I worked hard on the essay, but my private eye didn't comment on it. He just told me the job was easy. He said it would take one day. He said he'd locate the house, call and confirm George was still there, and that would be the end of it. But then I didn't hear back for a week.

Finally he wrote. "The case has complications. Things do not look good for George."

The house had been foreclosed on. Someone was suing him.

The news got worse and worse.

His company was no longer his company. Wherever he was, there seemed to be no wife with him, no child in sight. He might be living in New Mexico with his mother.

"Are you sure you have the right man?" I said. "That doesn't sound like George to have a company."

"Yes, he had a company. Translating INS documents."

"Oh," I said. "You have the right man."

Then he seemed to be fleeing too. That was suddenly part of it. The court couldn't serve him papers. He was last seen in Florida, no, New Mexico. There were other states involved. Wisconsin. Pennsylvania again. I could tell my private eye thought George was a deadbeat and wondered why I needed to know so much about an irresponsible reprobate. My private eye sounded disapproving. Meanwhile I mourned George and what had become of him, alone, living with his mother. What had happened? Had he found owning a company insipid? Was he lazy? I was certain he'd never learned how to pay a bill, but what about the queen? Had she been mean or insane? And what about the child? I regretted looking for George. He should be allowed his own private catastrophe.

I still believe in him, I thought loyally. I knew him when he was young, and I know he still is what he was then: patient and kind and brilliant. It shouldn't have turned out this way.

Then the story got better and better.

"There's no record of any divorce," my private eye told me. "In fact it's hard to figure out just who the wife is. There's a Brazilian woman who's shared a lot of addresses with him. Could that be the wife?

"People are protecting him, that's for sure," my private eye said. "He's in hiding. He's avoiding being served."

"He's had so many addresses in so many states," my private eye said, "it's impossible to follow it all." The business might now be in the Brazilian woman's name. The paperwork was convoluted.

New Mexico kept coming up, so I called the number the private eye gave me. A man answered the phone. "Is this George?" I said.

"I'm not George," he said.

I didn't think it was. I thought I would still know his voice, and anyway this voice sounded too young.

"Could you give him a message?"

"I don't know who you're talking about."

"I swear I'm not a bill collector."

"I'm not saying you are. I just don't know any George."

"I knew him in college. I need to get him the message."

"I could maybe get him a message."

"Could you tell him I'm not a bill collector?"

"All right."

"Ask him to call me."

"Give me your number."

"Write this down. It's like a password. He'll know who I am."

"Okay."

"Do you speak Spanish?"

"Not really," he said. "I speak Portuguese."

Ahhhhh. Brazil. My heart leapt. Was I talking to George's teenage son?

In that moment I had a flash of what had happened.

"Tell him: *Aquí no se rinde nadie*," I said. It was a Sandinista slogan. We used to say it all the time. Here no one surrenders.

George was not lost. In fact he had won. I'd figured it out. His wife had not deserted him, business gone broke. She was still with him, hiding his business for him. His son sounded like he loved him. He was the same George, up to his old tricks. He'd pulled one off on them all, he was running off into the sunset, leaving his trail of debt behind him, *Viva la revolución*, he will never surrender.

Indeed it was likely I who had more stuff.

He didn't call back, of course, but it was okay. I had what I needed. I was sitting on my bed in my apartment, water out the window, papers strewn all over the bed and the floor and the table and spread all over the stairs and the room beneath me and the counter in the kitchen, and suddenly my life seemed to have all the air sucked out of it, all my furniture, the care I'd taken in carrying it across the land and bringing it into this room. What did I care about? What was worth believing in? It was a tremendous feeling, glorious, that challenge to what I'd deemed important. I hadn't felt it in so long.

I don't know if I hired the private eye so I could write the book or if I wrote the book so I could hire the private eye, but I needed to know that George still existed, still exists, that the thing that he is *exists*, that it's out there somewhere, roaming the earth, creating havoc, growing, possibly multiplying. I want it to exist.

FINAL ROBBERY

George and I were in Mexico City, almost home, when we finally ran out of money. All the usual ways people outspend themselves were avenues not open to us. Nineteen eighty-seven was at the very beginning of the credit craze. I didn't have a credit card yet. George had defaulted on both of his. I think we had something like forty dollars. We talked about who would be more likely to give us money: my mother or his mother. The fathers were out of the question and we both hoped they didn't answer the phone. His mother had less money, but my mother always said no. I said I was willing to bet his mother could spare a few bucks. He said, "Let's ask your mom first." So I called my mother and she said no. She said that if we made it to the border she and my father would pick us up. I may not have admitted just how bad things had gotten. I like to think if I had been honest about the situation they would have come up with the cash. I'll never know.

But now we had no choice. George had to call his mother. She said she would wire us two hundred dollars. George went to pick it up at the cash express and was robbed coming back. A group of men got around him on the train, cut the money belt from his neck with a knife, and took his wallet. He was late coming back— I think he wound up walking partway. I'm not sure. He was very late and upset. He was shaking, and it took him a long time to calm down.

Then we kept saying, "Oh great," and throwing up our hands. "Now what are we going to do?" There was a horrible day or two when we didn't know how we were going to make it to the border. Then we made it to the border.

I mean, we didn't just live there for the rest of our lives.

ACKNOWLEDGMENTS

With heartfelt thanks to the following people for their vital assistance and friendship: Clancy Martin, Chris Miller, Ben Marcus, Diane Williams, Gillian Blake, Ethan Nosowsky, David McCormick, Kaydi and Cean Colcord, Robert Nelson, Rosalyn Olin Porte, Margaret Olin, Nancy Unferth, and, above all, Matt Evans.

Grateful thanks also to the Creative Capital Foundation and the Corporation of Yaddo, and to Eli Horowitz and *McSweeney's Internet Tendency*, where selections from this book originally appeared.

ABOUT THE AUTHOR

DEB OLIN UNFERTH is the author of the story collection *Minor Robberies* and the novel *Vacation*, winner of the 2009 Cabell First Novelist Award. Her work has been featured in *Harper's Magazine*, *McSweeney's*, *The Believer*, and the *Boston Review*. She has received two Pushcart Prizes and a 2009 Creative Capital grant for Innovative Literature. She teaches at Wesleyan University.

ABOUT THE AUTHOR

DEB OLIN UNFERTH is the author of the story collection *Minor Robberies* and the novel *Vacation*, winner of the 2009 Cabell First Novelist Award. Her work has been featured in *Harper's Magazine, McSweeney's, The Believer,* and the *Boston Review.* She has received two Pushcart Prizes and a 2009 Creative Capital grant for Innovative Literature. She teaches at Wesleyan University.